MznLnx

Missing Links Exam Preps

Exam Prep for

Matching Supply With Demand

Cachon, Terwiesch, 1st Edition

The MznLnx Exam Prep is your link from the texbook and lecture to your exams.
The MznLnx Exam Preps are unauthorized and comprehensive reviews of your textbooks.

All material provided by MznLnx and Rico Publications (c) 2010
Textbook publishers and textbook authors do not particpate in or contribute to these reviews.

MznLnx

Rico
Publications

Exam Prep for Matching Supply With Demand
1st Edition
Cachon, Terwiesch

Publisher: Raymond Houge
Assistant Editor: Michael Rouger
Text and Cover Designer: Lisa Buckner
Marketing Manager: Sara Swagger
Project Manager, Editorial Production: Jerry Emerson
Art Director: Vernon Lowerui

Product Manager: Dave Mason
Editorial Assitant: Rachel Guzmanji
Pedagogy: Debra Long
Cover Image: Jim Reed/Getty Images
Text and Cover Printer: City Printing, Inc.
Compositor: Media Mix, Inc.

(c) 2010 Rico Publications
ALL RIGHTS RESERVED. No part of this work covered by the copyright may be reproduced or used in any form or by an means--graphic, electronic, or mechanical, including photocopying, recording, taping, Web distribution, information storage, and retrieval systems, or in any other manner--without the written permission of the publisher.

Printed in the United States
ISBN:

For more information about our products, contact us at:
Dave.Mason@RicoPublications.com

For permission to use material from this text or product, submit a request online to:
Dave.Mason@RicoPublications.com

Contents

CHAPTER 1
The Process View of the Organization — 1

CHAPTER 2
Understanding the Supply Process: Evaluating Process Capacity — 8

CHAPTER 3
Estimating and Reducing Labor Costs — 9

CHAPTER 4
Batching and Other Flow Interruptions — 13

CHAPTER 5
Variability and Its Impact on Process Performance: Waiting Time Problems — 17

CHAPTER 6
The Impact of Variability on Process Performance: Throughput Losses — 25

CHAPTER 7
Quality Management and the Toyota Production System — 28

CHAPTER 8
Betting on Uncertain Demand: The Newsvendor Model — 36

CHAPTER 9
Assemble-to-Order, Make-to-Order, and Quick Response with Reactive Capacity — 45

CHAPTER 10
Service Levels and Lead Times in Supply Chains: The Order-up-to Inventory Model — 51

CHAPTER 11
Risk-Pooling Strategies to Reduce and Hedge Uncertainty — 59

CHAPTER 12
Revenue Management with Capacity Controls — 66

CHAPTER 13
Supply Chain Coordination — 69

ANSWER KEY — 83

TO THE STUDENT

COMPREHENSIVE

The *MznLnx* Exam Prep series is designed to help you pass your exams. Editors at MznLnx review your textbooks and then prepare these practice exams to help you master the textbook material. Unlike study guides, workbooks, and practice tests provided by the texbook publisher and textbook authors, *MznLnx* gives you **all** of the material in each chapter in exam form, not just samples, so you can be sure to nail your exam.

MECHANICAL

The MznLnx Exam Prep series creates exams that will help you learn the subject matter as well as test you on your understanding. Each question is designed to help you master the concept. Just working through the exams, you gain an understanding of the subject--its a simple mechanical process that produces success.

INTEGRATED STUDY GUIDE AND REVIEW

MznLnx is not just a set of exams designed to test you, its also a comprehensive review of the subject content. Each exam question is also a review of the concept, making sure that you will get the answer correct without having to go to other sources of material. You learn as you go! Its the easiest way to pass an exam.

HUMOR

Studying can be tedious and dry. MznLnx's instructional design includes moderate humor within the exam questions on occassion, to break the tedium and revitalize the brain

Chapter 1. The Process View of the Organization 1

1. _____, in marketing, manufacturing, call centres and management, is the use of flexible computer-aided manufacturing systems to produce custom output. Those systems combine the low unit costs of mass production processes with the flexibility of individual customization.

'_____' is the new frontier in business competition for both manufacturing and service industries.

   a. 1921 recession
   b. 130-30 fund
   c. 100-year flood
   d. Mass customization

2. _____ is one of the four Ps of the marketing mix. The other three aspects are product, promotion, and place. It is also a key variable in microeconomic price allocation theory.
   a. Pricing
   b. Premium pricing
   c. Point of total assumption
   d. Guaranteed Maximum Price

3. A _____ is a type of bar chart that illustrates a project schedule. _____s illustrate the start and finish dates of the terminal elements and summary elements of a project. Terminal elements and summary elements comprise the work breakdown structure of the project.
   a. 1921 recession
   b. 100-year flood
   c. Gantt chart
   d. 130-30 fund

4. _____ refers to the movement of cash into or out of a business or financial product. It is usually measured during a specified, finite period of time. Measurement of _____ can be used

   - to determine a project's rate of return or value. The time of _____s into and out of projects are used as inputs in financial models such as internal rate of return, and net present value.
   - to determine problems with a business's liquidity. Being profitable does not necessarily mean being liquid. A company can fail because of a shortage of cash, even while profitable.
   - as an alternate measure of a business's profits when it is believed that accrual accounting concepts do not represent economic realities. For example, a company may be notionally profitable but generating little operational cash (as may be the case for a company that barters its products rather than selling for cash.) In such a case, the company may be deriving additional operating cash by issuing shares evaluating default risk, re-investment requirements, etc.

_____ is a generic term used differently depending on the context. It may be defined by users for their own purposes.

Chapter 1. The Process View of the Organization

a. Second lien loan
b. Restricted stock
c. Strip financing
d. Cash flow

5. _____ is the discipline of planning, organizing and managing resources to bring about the successful completion of specific project goals and objectives.

A project is a finite endeavor--having specific start and completion dates--undertaken to meet particular goals and objectives, usually to bring about beneficial change or added value. This finite characteristic of projects stands in contrast to processes, or operations--which is repetitive, permanent or semi-permanent functional work to produce products or services.

a. 1921 recession
b. 130-30 fund
c. Project management
d. 100-year flood

6. The term _____, 'the state or characteristic of being variable', _____ describes how spread out or closely clustered a set of data is. may be applied to many different subjects:

- Climate _____
- Genetic _____
- Heart rate _____
- Human _____
- Solar van
- Spatial _____
- Statistical _____
- _____

a. Total product
b. Characteristic
c. Variability
d. Demand

7. _____ is the term denoting either an entrance or changes which are inserted into a system and which activate/modify a process. It is an abstract concept, used in the modeling, system(s) design and system(s) exploitation. It is usually connected with other terms, e.g., _____ field, _____ variable, _____ parameter, _____ value, _____ signal, _____ device and _____ file.

Chapter 1. The Process View of the Organization

a. ACCRA Cost of Living Index
b. ACEA agreement
c. AD-IA Model
d. Input

8. _____, or a _____ is the concept of a resulting effect (cf. cause and effect, arising from another action. In general terms, it is used to indicate that all human actions, particularly crime and sin, have profound effects.
   a. Variability
   b. Consequence
   c. Solved
   d. Rule

9. A _____ is an expression that compares quantities relative to each other. The most common examples involve two quantities, but any number of quantities can be compared. _____s are represented mathematically by separating each quantity with a colon, for example the _____ 2:3, which is read as the _____ 'two to three'.
   a. 100-year flood
   b. Y-intercept
   c. Ratio
   d. 130-30 fund

10. A _____ is something that is acted upon or used by or by human labor or industry, for use as a building material to create some product or structure. Often the term is used to denote material that came from nature and is in an unprocessed or minimally processed state. Iron ore, logs, and crude oil, would be examples.
    a. 130-30 fund
    b. 100-year flood
    c. 1921 recession
    d. Raw material

11. A _____ is an object whose consumption increases the utility of the consumer, for which the quantity demanded exceeds the quantity supplied at zero price. _____s are usually modeled as having diminishing marginal utility. The first individual purchase has high utility; the second has less.
    a. Merit good
    b. Pie method
    c. Composite good
    d. Good

12. In business management, _____ often referred to as stockturn, stock turns, turns, and stock turnover.

This measures the number of times invested in goods to be sold or used over in a year.

$$\text{Inventory Turns} = \frac{Cost\,of\,Goods\,Sold\,(over\,a\,given\,period)}{Average\,Inventory\,(for\,the\,period)}$$

An item whose inventory is sold (turns over) once a year has higher holding cost than one that turns over twice, or three times, or more in that time.

a. Inventory turns
b. AD-IA Model
c. ACCRA Cost of Living Index
d. ACEA agreement

13. In financial accounting, _____ or cost of sales includes the direct costs attributable to the production of the goods sold by a company. This amount includes the materials cost used in creating the goods along with the direct labour costs used to produce the good. It excludes indirect expenses such as distribution costs and sales force costs.
a. 100-year flood
b. 130-30 fund
c. 1921 recession
d. Cost of goods sold

14. _____, Gross profit margin or Gross Profit Rate can be defined as the amount of contribution to the business enterprise, after paying for direct-fixed and direct-variable unit costs, required to cover overheads (fixed commitments) and provide a buffer for unknown items. It expresses the relationship between gross profit and sales revenue.

It can be expressed in absolute terms:

Gross Profit = Revenue − Cost of Goods Sold

or as the ratio of gross profit to sales revenue, usually in the form of a percentage:

_____ Percentage = (Revenue-Cost of Goods Sold)/Revenue

Cost of goods sold includes variable costs and fixed costs directly linked to the product, such as material and labor.

Chapter 1. The Process View of the Organization 5

a. 100-year flood
b. Normal profit
c. Profit maximization
d. Gross margin

15. Network externalities resemble economies of scale, but they are not considered such because they are a function of the number of users of a good or service in an industry, not of the production efficiency within a business. _____ are only considered examples of network externalities if they are driven by demand side economies.

Formally, a production function $F(K, L)$ is defined to have:

- constant returns to scale if (for any constant a greater than or equal to 0) $F(aK, aL) = aF(K, L)$
- increasing returns to scale if (for any constant a greater than 1) $F(aK, aL) > aF(K, L)$,
- decreasing returns to scale if (for any constant a greater than 1) $F(aK, aL) < aF(K, L)$

where K and L are factors of production, capital and labour, respectively.

As an example, the Cobb-Douglas functional form has constant returns to scale when the sum of the exponents adds up to one.

a. AD-IA Model
b. ACCRA Cost of Living Index
c. ACEA agreement
d. Economies of scale external to the firm

16. Economics:

- _____ ,the desire to own something and the ability to pay for it
- _____ curve, a graphic representation of a _____ schedule
- _____ deposit, the money in checking accounts
- _____ pull theory, the theory that inflation occurs when _____ for goods and services exceeds existing supplies
- _____ schedule, a table that lists the quantity of a good a person will buy it each different price
- _____ side economics, the school of economics at believes government spending and tax cuts open economy by raising _____

a. Production
b. Demand
c. McKesson ' Robbins scandal
d. Variability

17. In statistics, many time series exhibit cyclic variation known as _____, periodic variation, or periodic fluctuations. This variation can be either regular or semiregular.

For example, retail sales tend to peak for the Christmas season and then decline after the holidays.

a. Trispectrum
b. Seasonal adjustment
c. Seasonality
d. Linear prediction

18. _____ means random.

A _____ process is one whose behavior is non-deterministic in that a system's subsequent state is determined both by the process's predictable actions and by a random element. _____ crafts are complex systems whose practitioners, even if complete experts, acknowledge that outcomes result from both known and unknown causes.

a. 130-30 fund
b. Theory
c. 100-year flood
d. Stochastic

19. _____ are typically small manufacturing operations that handle specialized manufacturing processes such as small customer orders or small batch jobs. _____ typically move on to different jobs (possibly with different customers) when each job is completed. By nature of this type of manufacturing operation, _____ are usually specialized in skill and processes.

a. 130-30 fund
b. Job shops
c. Product binning
d. 100-year flood

20. _____ was the American founder of the Ford Motor Company and father of modern assembly lines used in mass production. His introduction of the Model T automobile revolutionized transportation and American industry. He was a prolific inventor and was awarded 161 U.S. patents.
   a. George Cabot Lodge II
   b. Henry Ford
   c. Maximilian Carl Emil Weber
   d. Werner Sombart

Chapter 2. Understanding the Supply Process: Evaluating Process Capacity

1. _____ is often a synonym for chemical engineering and focuses on the design, operation and maintenance of chemical and material manufacturing processes. _____ and process engineers are found in a vast range of industries, such as the petrochemical, mineral processing, material, Information Technology, food and pharmaceutical and biotechnological industries. _____ also involves developing new processes, project engineering and troubleshooting.
    a. 130-30 fund
    b. 100-year flood
    c. Clean coal technology
    d. Process engineering

2. A _____ is a type of bar chart that illustrates a project schedule. _____s illustrate the start and finish dates of the terminal elements and summary elements of a project. Terminal elements and summary elements comprise the work breakdown structure of the project.
    a. 130-30 fund
    b. 100-year flood
    c. 1921 recession
    d. Gantt chart

3. _____ is a concept in economics which refers to the extent to which an enterprise or a nation actually uses its installed productive capacity. Thus, it refers to the relationship between actual output that 'is' produced with the installed equipment and the potential output which 'could' be produced with it, if capacity was fully used.

If market demand grows, _____ will rise.

   a. Long-run
   b. Capacity utilization
   c. Diseconomies of scale
   d. Marginal product of labor

Chapter 3. Estimating and Reducing Labor Costs

1. Economics:

    - _____, the desire to own something and the ability to pay for it
    - _____ curve, a graphic representation of a _____ schedule
    - _____ deposit, the money in checking accounts
    - _____ pull theory, the theory that inflation occurs when _____ for goods and services exceeds existing supplies
    - _____ schedule, a table that lists the quantity of a good a person will buy it each different price
    - _____ side economics, the school of economics at believes government spending and tax cuts open economy by raising _____

    a. Production
    b. McKesson ' Robbins scandal
    c. Demand
    d. Variability

2. A _____ is an object whose consumption increases the utility of the consumer, for which the quantity demanded exceeds the quantity supplied at zero price. _____s are usually modeled as having diminishing marginal utility. The first individual purchase has high utility; the second has less.
    a. Good
    b. Pie method
    c. Merit good
    d. Composite good

3. In calculus, a function f defined on a subset of the real numbers with real values is called _____, if for all x and y such that $x \geq y$ one has $f(x) \geq f(y)$, so f preserves the order. In layman's terms, the sign of the slope is always positive (the curve tending upwards) or zero (i.e., non-decreasing, or asymptotic, or depicted as a horizontal, flat line) Likewise, a function is called monotonically decreasing (non-increasing) if, whenever $x \geq y$, then $f(x) \geq f(y)$, so it reverses the order.
    a. 100-year flood
    b. Monotonic
    c. 130-30 fund
    d. 1921 recession

4. In finance, the _____ of a financial asset measures the sensitivity of the asset's price to interest rate movements. There are various definitions of _____ and derived quantities, discussed below. If not otherwise specified, '_____' generally means the Macaulay _____, as defined below.

Chapter 3. Estimating and Reducing Labor Costs

a. Time value of money
b. Duration
c. Newtonian time
d. 100-year flood

5. In microeconomics, _____ is quite simply the conversion of inputs into outputs. It is an economic process that uses resources to create a good or service that is suitable for exchange. This can include manufacturing, storing, shipping, and packaging.

   a. Red Guards
   b. Solved
   c. Production
   d. MET

6. An _____ is a manufacturing process in which parts (usually interchangeable parts) are added to a product in a sequential manner using optimally planned logistics to create a finished product much faster than with handcrafting-type methods. The _____ developed by Ford Motor Company between 1908 and 1915 made _____ s famous in the following decade through the social ramifications of mass production, such as the affordability of the Ford Model T and the introduction of high wages for Ford workers. However, the various preconditions for the development at Ford stretched far back into the 19th century, from the gradual realization of the dream of interchangeability, to the concept of reinventing workflow and job descriptions using analytical methods.

   a. Assembly line
   b. ACCRA Cost of Living Index
   c. ACEA agreement
   d. AD-IA Model

7. The _____ is a system for calculating margin requirements for futures and options on futures. It was developed by the Chicago Mercantile Exchange in 1988.

SPAN is a portfolio margining method that uses grid simulation.

   a. Callable bull/bear contract
   b. Repurchase agreement
   c. Standard Portfolio Analysis of Risk
   d. Volatility swap

8. _____ is a term originating in military organization theory, but now used more commonly in business management, particularly human resource management. _____ refers to the number of subordinates a supervisor has.

Chapter 3. Estimating and Reducing Labor Costs

In the hierarchical business organization of the past it was not uncommon to see average spans of 1 to 10 or even less.

a. Codetermination
b. Cash cow
c. Span of control
d. Business plan

9. _____ is the acquisition of goods and/or services at the best possible total cost of ownership, in the right quantity and quality, at the right time, in the right place and from the right source for the direct benefit or use of corporations or individuals, generally via a contract. Simple _____ may involve nothing more than repeat purchasing. Complex _____ could involve finding long term partners - or even 'co-destiny' suppliers that might fundamentally commit one organization to another.

a. Golden umbrella
b. Sole proprietorship
c. Pre-emerging markets
d. Procurement

10. _____ refers to a business or organization attempting to acquire goods or services to accomplish the goals of the enterprise. Though there are several organizations that attempt to set standards in the _____ process, processes can vary greatly between organizations. Typically the word '_____' is not used interchangeably with the word 'procurement', since procurement typically includes Expediting, Supplier Quality, and Traffic and Logistics (T'L) in addition to _____.

a. 100-year flood
b. Purchasing
c. 130-30 fund
d. Free port

11. Modern portfolio theory (MPT) proposes how rational investors will use diversification to optimize their portfolios, and how a risky asset should be priced. The basic concepts of the theory are Markowitz diversification, the _____, capital asset pricing model, the alpha and beta coefficients, the Capital Market Line and the Securities Market Line.

MPT models an asset's return as a random variable, and models a portfolio as a weighted combination of assets so that the return of a portfolio is the weighted combination of the assets' returns.

a. ACEA agreement
b. ACCRA Cost of Living Index
c. AD-IA Model
d. Efficient frontier

12. A _____ is a method for transporting items where items are passed from one stationary person to the next. More specifically, it refers to a method of firefighting before the advent of hand pumped fire engines, whereby firefighters would pass buckets to each other to extinguish a blaze. A famous example of this is the Union Fire Company.
    a. 100-year flood
    b. 1921 recession
    c. 130-30 fund
    d. Bucket brigade

Chapter 4. Batching and Other Flow Interruptions

1. _____ is the production of large amounts of standardized products, including and especially on assembly lines. The concepts of _____ are applied to various kinds of products, from fluids and particulates handled in bulk to discrete solid parts to assemblies of such parts

_____ of assemblies typically uses electric-motor-powered moving tracks or conveyor belts to move partially complete products to workers, who perform simple repetitive tasks.

   a. 130-30 fund
   b. 100-year flood
   c. Mass production
   d. 1921 recession

2. In microeconomics, _____ is quite simply the conversion of inputs into outputs. It is an economic process that uses resources to create a good or service that is suitable for exchange. This can include manufacturing, storing, shipping, and packaging.
   a. Solved
   b. Production
   c. MET
   d. Red Guards

3. _____: A distribution term that refers to the status of items on a purchase order in the event that some or all of the inventory required to fulfill the order is insufficient to satisfy demand. This differs from a forward order where stock is available but delivery is postponed for another reason.

_____ Cost: A cost incurred by a business when it is unable to fill an order and must complete it later.

   a. Backorder
   b. Centralization
   c. Poverty penalty
   d. Teaser rate

4. Modern portfolio theory (MPT) proposes how rational investors will use diversification to optimize their portfolios, and how a risky asset should be priced. The basic concepts of the theory are Markowitz diversification, the _____, capital asset pricing model, the alpha and beta coefficients, the Capital Market Line and the Securities Market Line.

MPT models an asset's return as a random variable, and models a portfolio as a weighted combination of assets so that the return of a portfolio is the weighted combination of the assets' returns.

Chapter 4. Batching and Other Flow Interruptions

   a. AD-IA Model
   b. ACCRA Cost of Living Index
   c. Efficient frontier
   d. ACEA agreement

5. _____s is the social science that studies the production, distribution, and consumption of goods and services. The term _____s comes from the Ancient Greek oá¼°κονομῖα from oá¼¶κος (oikos, 'house') + νΐŒμος (nomos, 'custom' or 'law'), hence 'rules of the house(hold)'. Current _____ models developed out of the broader field of political economy in the late 19th century, owing to a desire to use an empirical approach more akin to the physical sciences.
   a. Opportunity cost
   b. Inflation
   c. Energy economics
   d. Economic

6. _____ is the level of inventory that minimizes the total inventory holding costs and ordering costs. The framework used to determine this order quantity is also known as Wilson _____ Model. The model was developed by F. W. Harris in 1913.
   a. Economic order quantity
   b. AD-IA Model
   c. ACCRA Cost of Living Index
   d. ACEA agreement

7. _____ is the acquisition of goods and/or services at the best possible total cost of ownership, in the right quantity and quality, at the right time, in the right place and from the right source for the direct benefit or use of corporations or individuals, generally via a contract. Simple _____ may involve nothing more than repeat purchasing. Complex _____ could involve finding long term partners - or even 'co-destiny' suppliers that might fundamentally commit one organization to another.
   a. Sole proprietorship
   b. Golden umbrella
   c. Procurement
   d. Pre-emerging markets

8. _____ refers to a business or organization attempting to acquire goods or services to accomplish the goals of the enterprise. Though there are several organizations that attempt to set standards in the _____ process, processes can vary greatly between organizations. Typically the word '_____' is not used interchangeably with the word 'procurement', since procurement typically includes Expediting, Supplier Quality, and Traffic and Logistics (T'L) in addition to _____.

Chapter 4. Batching and Other Flow Interruptions 15

a. 100-year flood
b. Purchasing
c. Free port
d. 130-30 fund

9. _____, in microeconomics, are the cost advantages that a business obtains due to expansion. They are factors that cause a producere;s average cost per unit to fall as scale is increased. _____ is a long run concept and refers to reductions in unit cost as the size of a facility, or scale, increases.

   a. Economies of scale
   b. Isoquant
   c. Economic production quantity
   d. Underinvestment employment relationship

10. _____ is the state of being which occurs when a person, object, or service is no longer wanted even though it may still be in good working order. _____ frequently occurs because a replacement has become available that is superior in one or more aspects. Videotapes making way for DVDs

Technical _____ may occur when a new product or technology supersedes the old, and it becomes preferred to utilize the new technology in place of the old.

   a. Obsolescence
   b. ACEA agreement
   c. ACCRA Cost of Living Index
   d. AD-IA Model

11. Network externalities resemble economies of scale, but they are not considered such because they are a function of the number of users of a good or service in an industry, not of the production efficiency within a business. _____ are only considered examples of network externalities if they are driven by demand side economies.

Formally, a production function $F(K, L)$ is defined to have:

- constant returns to scale if (for any constant a greater than or equal to 0) $F(aK, aL) = aF(K, L)$
- increasing returns to scale if (for any constant a greater than 1) $F(aK, aL) > aF(K, L)$,
- decreasing returns to scale if (for any constant a greater than 1) $F(aK, aL) < aF(K, L)$

where K and L are factors of production, capital and labour, respectively.

Chapter 4. Batching and Other Flow Interruptions

As an example, the Cobb-Douglas functional form has constant returns to scale when the sum of the exponents adds up to one.

   a. ACCRA Cost of Living Index
   b. ACEA agreement
   c. AD-IA Model
   d. Economies of scale external to the firm

12. Discounting is a financial mechanism in which a debtor obtains the right to delay payments to a creditor, for a defined period of time, in exchange for a charge or fee. Essentially, the party that owes money in the present purchases the right to delay the payment until some future date. The _____, or charge, is simply the difference between the original amount owed in the present and the amount that has to be paid in the future to settle the debt.

   a. Reliability theory
   b. Reinsurance
   c. Discount
   d. Certified Risk Manager

13. _____ varies from Process Manufacturing. In _____, the manufacturing floor works off orders to build something. Examples include toys, medical equipment, computers and cars.

   a. Homeworkers
   b. Flexible manufacturing
   c. Vendor lock-in
   d. Discrete manufacturing

14. _____ is one of the many lean production methods for reducing waste in a manufacturing process. It provides a rapid and efficient way of converting a manufacturing process from running the current product to running the next product. This rapid changeover is key to reducing production lot sizes and thereby improving flow ' href='/wiki/Mura_'>Mura) The phrase 'single minute' does not mean that all changeovers and startups should take only one minute, but that they should take less than 10 minutes (in other words, 'single digit minute'.)

   a. 100-year flood
   b. Process capability
   c. Statistical process control
   d. Single minute exchange of die

Chapter 5. Variability and Its Impact on Process Performance: Waiting Time Problems

1. Economics:

    - _____, the desire to own something and the ability to pay for it
    - _____ curve, a graphic representation of a _____ schedule
    - _____ deposit, the money in checking accounts
    - _____ pull theory, the theory that inflation occurs when _____ for goods and services exceeds existing supplies
    - _____ schedule, a table that lists the quantity of a good a person will buy it each different price
    - _____ side economics, the school of economics at believes government spending and tax cuts open economy by raising _____

    a. Production
    b. Variability
    c. McKesson ' Robbins scandal
    d. Demand

2. The term _____, 'the state or characteristic of being variable', _____ describes how spread out or closely clustered a set of data is. may be applied to many different subjects:

    - Climate _____
    - Genetic _____
    - Heart rate _____
    - Human _____
    - Solar van
    - Spatial _____
    - Statistical _____
    - _____

    a. Total product
    b. Variability
    c. Characteristic
    d. Demand

3. Necessary _____s:

If x is a necessary _____ of y, then the presence of y necessarily implies the presence of x. The presence of x, however, does not imply that y will occur.

Sufficient _____s:

If x is a sufficient _____ of y, then the presence of x necessarily implies the presence of y.

Chapter 5. Variability and Its Impact on Process Performance: Waiting Time Problems

a. Political philosophy
b. Materialism
c. Philosophy of economics
d. Cause

4. _____ is the process of understanding, anticipating and influencing consumer behavior in order to maximize revenue or profits from a fixed, perishable resource This process was first discovered by Dr. Matt H. Keller. The challenge is to sell the right resources to the right customer at the right time for the right price.

a. Freebie marketing
b. Subscription
c. Coopetition
d. Yield management

5. A _____ is a type of bar chart that illustrates a project schedule. _____s illustrate the start and finish dates of the terminal elements and summary elements of a project. Terminal elements and summary elements comprise the work breakdown structure of the project.

a. 1921 recession
b. 100-year flood
c. 130-30 fund
d. Gantt chart

6. _____ is a concept with somewhat disparate meanings in several fields. It also has a common meaning which has a loose connection with some of those more definite meanings.

Casually, it is typically used to denote a lack of order, or purpose, or cause.

a. 100-year flood
b. 130-30 fund
c. 1921 recession
d. Randomness

7. In probability theory and statistics, _____ is a measure of the variability or dispersion of a population, a data set, or a probability distribution. A low _____ indicates that the data points tend to be very close to the same value (the mean), while high _____ indicates that the data are 'spread out' over a large range of values.

For example, the average height for adult men in the United States is about 70 inches, with a _____ of around 3 inches.

Chapter 5. Variability and Its Impact on Process Performance: Waiting Time Problems

a. Standard deviation
b. 100-year flood
c. 1921 recession
d. 130-30 fund

8. In mathematics, a _____ is a constant multiplicative factor of a certain object. For example, in the expression $9x^2$, the _____ of x^2 is 9.

The object can be such things as a variable, a vector, a function, etc.

a. 100-year flood
b. 1921 recession
c. 130-30 fund
d. Coefficient

9. In mathematics, _____ are used in the study of chance and probability. They were developed to assist in the analysis of games of chance, stochastic events, and the results of scientific experiments by capturing only the mathematical properties necessary to answer probabilistic questions. Further formalizations have firmly grounded the entity in the theoretical domains of mathematics by making use of measure theory.

a. 100-year flood
b. 130-30 fund
c. 1921 recession
d. Random variables

10. In statistics, many time series exhibit cyclic variation known as _____, periodic variation, or periodic fluctuations. This variation can be either regular or semiregular.

For example, retail sales tend to peak for the Christmas season and then decline after the holidays.

a. Seasonality
b. Trispectrum
c. Linear prediction
d. Seasonal adjustment

11. In probability theory and statistics, the _____ or just distribution function, completely describes the probability distribution of a real-valued random variable X. For every real number x, the _____ of X is given by

Chapter 5. Variability and Its Impact on Process Performance: Waiting Time Problems

$$x \mapsto F_X(x) = P(X \leq x),$$

where the right-hand side represents the probability that the random variable X takes on a value less than or equal to x. The probability that X lies in the interval (a, b] is therefore $F_X(b) - F_X(a)$ if a < b.

If treating several random variables X, Y, ...

a. Cumulative distribution function
b. 100-year flood
c. 130-30 fund
d. 1921 recession

12. In molecular kinetic theory in physics, a particle's _____ is a function of seven variables, $f(x,y,z,t;v_x,v_y,v_z)$, which gives the number of particles per unit volume in phase space. It is the number of particles having approximately the velocity (v_x,v_y,v_z) near the place (x,y,z) and time (t). The usual normalization of the _____ is

$$n(x, y, z, t) = \int f \, dv_x \, dv_y \, dv_z$$

$$N(t) = \int n \, dx \, dy \, dz$$

Here, N is the total number of particles and n is the number density of particles - the number of particles per unit volume, or the density divided by the mass of individual particles.

a. 100-year flood
b. 130-30 fund
c. 1921 recession
d. Distribution function

13. In probability theory, _____ is a property of certain probability distributions: the exponential distributions and the geometric distributions, wherein any derived probability from a set of random samples is distinct and has no information (i.e. 'memory') of earlier samples.

Suppose X is a discrete random variable whose values lie in the set { 0, 1, 2, ... }.

a. Marginal likelihood
b. Markov blanket
c. Graphical model
d. Memorylessness

14. In statistics, an _____ is a cumulative probability distribution function that concentrates probability 1/n at each of the n numbers in a sample.

Let $X_1, \ldots, X_n$ be iid real random variables with the cdf F(x.) The _____ $\hat{F}_n(x)$ is a step function defined by

$$\hat{F}_n(x) = \frac{\text{number of elements in the sample} \leq x}{n} = \frac{1}{n}\sum_{i=1}^{n} I(X_i \leq x),$$

where I(A) is the indicator of event A.

a. ACCRA Cost of Living Index
b. Empirical distribution function
c. AD-IA Model
d. ACEA agreement

15. In statistics, _____ has two related meanings:

- the arithmetic _____
- the expected value of a random variable, which is also called the population _____.

It is sometimes stated that the '_____' _____s average. This is incorrect if '_____' is taken in the specific sense of 'arithmetic _____' as there are different types of averages: the _____, median, and mode. Other simple statistical analyses use measures of spread, such as range, interquartile range, or standard deviation. For a real-valued random variable X, the _____ is the expectation of X. Note that not every probability distribution has a defined _____ (or variance); see the Cauchy distribution for an example.

a. 100-year flood
b. 1921 recession
c. 130-30 fund
d. Mean

Chapter 5. Variability and Its Impact on Process Performance: Waiting Time Problems

16. In mathematics, a _____ system is a system which is not linear, that is, a system which does not satisfy the superposition principle, or whose output is not proportional to its input. Less technically, a _____ system is any problem where the variable(s) to be solved for cannot be written as a linear combination of independent components. A nonhomogeneous system, which is linear apart from the presence of a function of the independent variables, is _____ according to a strict definition, but such systems are usually studied alongside linear systems, because they can be transformed to a linear system of multiple variables.
   a. Nonlinear
   b. 100-year flood
   c. 130-30 fund
   d. Nonlinear system

17. _____, or a _____ is the concept of a resulting effect (cf. cause and effect, arising from another action. In general terms, it is used to indicate that all human actions, particularly crime and sin, have profound effects.
   a. Consequence
   b. Solved
   c. Rule
   d. Variability

18. _____s is the social science that studies the production, distribution, and consumption of goods and services. The term _____s comes from the Ancient Greek οἰκονομία from οἶκος (oikos, 'house') + νόμος (nomos, 'custom' or 'law'), hence 'rules of the house(hold)'. Current _____ models developed out of the broader field of political economy in the late 19th century, owing to a desire to use an empirical approach more akin to the physical sciences.
   a. Inflation
   b. Economic
   c. Energy economics
   d. Opportunity cost

Chapter 5. Variability and Its Impact on Process Performance: Waiting Time Problems   23

19. A _____ is:

- Rewrite _____, in generative grammar and computer science
- Standardization, a formal and widely-accepted statement, fact, definition, or qualification
- Operation, a determinate _____ for performing a mathematical operation and obtaining a certain result (Mathematics, Logic)
    - Unary operation
    - Binary operation
- _____ of inference, a function from sets of formulae to formulae (Mathematics, Logic)
- _____ of thumb, principle with broad application that is not intended to be strictly accurate or reliable for every situation. Also often simply referred to as a _____
- Moral, an atomic element of a moral code for guiding choices in human behavior
- Heuristic, a quantized '_____' which shows a tendency or probability for successful function
- A regulation, as in sports
- A Production _____, as in computer science
- Procedural law, a _____ set governing the application of laws to cases
    - A law, which may informally be called a '_____'
    - A court ruling, a decision by a court
- In the U.S. Government, a regulation mandated by Congress, but written or expanded upon by the Executive Branch.
- Norm (sociology), an informal but widely accepted _____, concept, truth, definition, or qualification (social norms, legal norms, coding norms)
- Norm (philosophy), a kind of sentence or a reason to act, feel or believe
- 'Rulership' is the concept of governance by a government:
    - Military _____, governance by a military body
    - Monastic _____, a collection of precepts that guides the life of monks or nuns in a religious order where the superior holds the place of Christ
- Slide _____

- '_____,' a song by Ayumi Hamasaki
- '_____,' a song by rapper Nas
- '_____s,' an album by the band The Whitest Boy Alive
- _____s: Pyaar Ka Superhit Formula, a 2003 Bollywood film
- ruler, an instrument for measuring lengths
- _____, a component of an astrolabe, circumferator or similar instrument
- The _____s, a bestselling self-help book
- _____ Project (Run Up-to-date Linux Everywhere), a project that aims to use up-to-date Linux software on old PCs
- _____ engine, a software system that helps managing business _____s
- Ja _____, a hip hop artist
    - R.U.L.E., a 2005 greatest hits album by rapper Ja _____
- '_____s,' a KMFDM song

Chapter 5. Variability and Its Impact on Process Performance: Waiting Time Problems

a. Demand
b. Procter ' Gamble
c. Technocracy
d. Rule

20. First-come, first-served (sometimes first-in, first-served, first-come, first choice or simply _____) is a service policy where by the requests of customers or clients are attended to in the order that they arrived, without other biases or preferences. The policy can be employed when processing sales orders, in determining restaurant seating, or on a taxi stand, for example.

Festival seating (also known as general seating and stadium seating) is seating done on a _____ basis.

a. FCFS
b. 100-year flood
c. 1921 recession
d. 130-30 fund

21. _____ is a service policy where by the requests of customers or clients are attended to in the order that they arrived, without other biases or preferences. The policy can be employed when processing sales orders, in determining restaurant seating, or on a taxi stand, for example.

Festival seating (also known as general seating and stadium seating) is seating done on a FCFS basis.

a. 1921 recession
b. First-come, first-served
c. 100-year flood
d. 130-30 fund

Chapter 6. The Impact of Variability on Process Performance: Throughput Losses

1. _____ is a formula for the blocking probability derived from the Erlang distribution to describe the probability of call loss on a group of circuits It is, for example, used in planning telephone networks. The formula was derived by Agner Krarup Erlang and is not limited to telephone networks, since it describes a probability in a queuing system
    a. AD-IA Model
    b. ACEA agreement
    c. ACCRA Cost of Living Index
    d. Erlang-B

2. _____ is an operational activity which does an aggregate plan for the production process, in advance of 2 to 18 months, to give an idea to management as to what quantity of materials and other resources are to be procured and when, so that the total cost of operations of the organization is kept to the minimum over that period.

    The quantity of outsourcing, subcontracting of items, overtime of labor, numbers to be hired and fired in each period and the amount of inventory to be held in stock and to be backlogged for each period are decided. All of these activities are done within the framework of the company ethics, policies, and long term commitment to the society, community and the country of operation.

    a. Aggregate planning
    b. ACCRA Cost of Living Index
    c. AD-IA Model
    d. ACEA agreement

3. In mathematics, a _____ is a constant multiplicative factor of a certain object. For example, in the expression $9x^2$, the _____ of x^2 is 9.

    The object can be such things as a variable, a vector, a function, etc.

    a. 100-year flood
    b. 130-30 fund
    c. 1921 recession
    d. Coefficient

4. _____ is a way of expressing knowledge or belief that an event will occur or has occurred. In mathematics the concept has been given an exact meaning in _____ theory, that is used extensively in such areas of study as mathematics, statistics, finance, gambling, science, and philosophy to draw conclusions about the likelihood of potential events and the underlying mechanics of complex systems.

    The word _____ does not have a consistent direct definition.

Chapter 6. The Impact of Variability on Process Performance: Throughput Losses

a. 130-30 fund
b. Probability
c. 1921 recession
d. 100-year flood

5. The term _____, 'the state or characteristic of being variable', _____ describes how spread out or closely clustered a set of data is. may be applied to many different subjects:

- Climate _____
- Genetic _____
- Heart rate _____
- Human _____
- Solar van
- Spatial _____
- Statistical _____
- _____

a. Characteristic
b. Demand
c. Total product
d. Variability

6. In statistics, decision theory and economics, a _____ is a function that maps an event (technically an element of a sample space) onto a real number representing the economic cost or regret associated with the event.

Less technically, in statistics a _____ represents the loss (cost in money or loss in utility in some other sense) associated with an estimate being 'wrong' (different from either a desired or a true value) as a function of a measure of the degree of wrongness (generally the difference between the estimated value and the true or desired value.)

Both Frequentist and Bayesian statistical theory involve calculating statistics in such a way as to minimize the expected loss observed from being wrong given a set of assumptions about the data and one's _____.

a. Population modeling
b. 100-year flood
c. Window function
d. Loss Function

Chapter 6. The Impact of Variability on Process Performance: Throughput Losses

7. Network externalities resemble economies of scale, but they are not considered such because they are a function of the number of users of a good or service in an industry, not of the production efficiency within a business. _____ are only considered examples of network externalities if they are driven by demand side economies.

Formally, a production function $F(K, L)$ is defined to have:

- constant returns to scale if (for any constant a greater than or equal to 0) $F(aK, aL) = aF(K, L)$
- increasing returns to scale if (for any constant a greater than 1) $F(aK, aL) > aF(K, L)$,
- decreasing returns to scale if (for any constant a greater than 1) $F(aK, aL) < aF(K, L)$

where K and L are factors of production, capital and labour, respectively.

As an example, the Cobb-Douglas functional form has constant returns to scale when the sum of the exponents adds up to one.

a. Economies of scale external to the firm
b. ACEA agreement
c. ACCRA Cost of Living Index
d. AD-IA Model

8. _____, or a _____ is the concept of a resulting effect (cf. cause and effect, arising from another action. In general terms, it is used to indicate that all human actions, particularly crime and sin, have profound effects.

a. Rule
b. Consequence
c. Solved
d. Variability

Chapter 7. Quality Management and the Toyota Production System

1. _____ is a concept related to lean and just-in-time (JIT) production. The Japanese word _____ is a common term meaning 'signboard' or 'billboard'. According to Taiichi Ohno, the man credited with developing JIT, _____ is a means through which JIT is achieved.
   a. Penny stock
   b. Kanban
   c. Risk management
   d. Non-disclosure agreement

2. _____ can be considered to have three main components: quality control, quality assurance and quality improvement. _____ is focused not only on product quality, but also the means to achieve it. _____ therefore uses quality assurance and control of processes as well as products to achieve more consistent quality.
   a. Quality management
   b. 130-30 fund
   c. 100-year flood
   d. 1921 recession

3. _____ is a business management strategy, initially implemented by Motorola, that today enjoys widespread application in many sectors of industry.

   _____ seeks to improve the quality of process outputs by identifying and removing the causes of defects (errors) and variation in manufacturing and business processes. It uses a set of quality management methods, including statistical methods, and creates a special infrastructure of people within the organization ('Black Belts' etc.)

   a. Primary sector of the economy
   b. Private sector
   c. Tertiary sector of economy
   d. Six sigma

4. _____ is an effective method of monitoring a process through the use of control charts. Control charts enable the use of objective criteria for distinguishing background variation from events of significance based on statistical techniques. Much of its power lies in the ability to monitor both process center and its variation about that center.
   a. 100-year flood
   b. Process capability
   c. Single minute exchange of die
   d. Statistical process control

Chapter 7. Quality Management and the Toyota Production System

5. _____ is a way of expressing knowledge or belief that an event will occur or has occurred. In mathematics the concept has been given an exact meaning in _____ theory, that is used extensively in such areas of study as mathematics, statistics, finance, gambling, science, and philosophy to draw conclusions about the likelihood of potential events and the underlying mechanics of complex systems.

The word _____ does not have a consistent direct definition.

a. 1921 recession
b. 130-30 fund
c. 100-year flood
d. Probability

6. Necessary _____s:

If x is a necessary _____ of y, then the presence of y necessarily implies the presence of x. The presence of x, however, does not imply that y will occur.

Sufficient _____s:

If x is a sufficient _____ of y, then the presence of x necessarily implies the presence of y.

a. Philosophy of economics
b. Cause
c. Political philosophy
d. Materialism

7. In microeconomics, _____ is quite simply the conversion of inputs into outputs. It is an economic process that uses resources to create a good or service that is suitable for exchange. This can include manufacturing, storing, shipping, and packaging.
a. MET
b. Production
c. Solved
d. Red Guards

8. In industrial statistics, the _____ is a type of control chart that is used to monitor the arithmetic means of successive samples of constant size, n. This type of control chart is used for characteristics that can be measured on a continuous scale, such as weight, temperature, thickness etc.

For the purposes of control limit calculation, the sample means are assumed to be normally distributed, an assumption justified by the Central Limit Theorem.

Chapter 7. Quality Management and the Toyota Production System

a. Partial regression plot
b. Partial residual plot
c. Smoothing
d. X-bar chart

9. The _____ is a measurable property of a process to the specification, expressed as a _____ index (e.g., C_{pk} or C_{pm}) or as a process performance index (e.g., P_{pk} or P_{pm}.) The output of this measurement is usually illustrated by a histogram and calculations that predict how many parts will be produced out of specification.

_____ is also defined as the capability of a process to meet its purpose as managed by an organization's management and process definition structures ISO 15504.

a. 100-year flood
b. Single minute exchange of die
c. Statistical process control
d. Process capability

10. _____ are horizontal lines drawn on an statistical process control chart, usually at a distance of ±3 standard deviations of the plotted statistic from the statistic's mean.

For normally distributed statistics, the area bracketed by the _____ will on average contain 99.73% of all the plot points on the chart, as long as the process is and remains in statistical control.

_____ should not be confused with tolerance limits, which are completely independent of the distribution of the plotted sample statistic.

a. 130-30 fund
b. 100-year flood
c. 1921 recession
d. Control limits

11. In probability theory and statistics, _____ is a measure of the variability or dispersion of a population, a data set, or a probability distribution. A low _____ indicates that the data points tend to be very close to the same value (the mean), while high _____ indicates that the data are 'spread out' over a large range of values.

For example, the average height for adult men in the United States is about 70 inches, with a _____ of around 3 inches.

Chapter 7. Quality Management and the Toyota Production System

a. 1921 recession
b. Standard deviation
c. 100-year flood
d. 130-30 fund

12. The term _____, 'the state or characteristic of being variable', _____ describes how spread out or closely clustered a set of data is. may be applied to many different subjects:

- Climate _____
- Genetic _____
- Heart rate _____
- Human _____
- Solar van
- Spatial _____
- Statistical _____
- _____

a. Variability
b. Total product
c. Characteristic
d. Demand

13. Economics:

- _____, the desire to own something and the ability to pay for it
- _____ curve, a graphic representation of a _____ schedule
- _____ deposit, the money in checking accounts
- _____ pull theory, the theory that inflation occurs when _____ for goods and services exceeds existing supplies
- _____ schedule, a table that lists the quantity of a good a person will buy it each different price
- _____ side economics, the school of economics at believes government spending and tax cuts open economy by raising _____

a. Production
b. Variability
c. McKesson ' Robbins scandal
d. Demand

Chapter 7. Quality Management and the Toyota Production System

14. Modern portfolio theory (MPT) proposes how rational investors will use diversification to optimize their portfolios, and how a risky asset should be priced. The basic concepts of the theory are Markowitz diversification, the _____, capital asset pricing model, the alpha and beta coefficients, the Capital Market Line and the Securities Market Line.

MPT models an asset's return as a random variable, and models a portfolio as a weighted combination of assets so that the return of a portfolio is the weighted combination of the assets' returns.

a. ACEA agreement
b. ACCRA Cost of Living Index
c. AD-IA Model
d. Efficient frontier

15. The _____ states that, for many events, roughly 80% of the effects come from 20% of the causes. Business management thinker Joseph M. Juran suggested the principle and named it after Italian economist Vilfredo Pareto, who observed that 80% of the land in Italy was owned by 20% of the population. It is a common rule of thumb in business; e.g., '80% of your sales come from 20% of your clients.' Mathematically, where something is shared among a sufficiently large set of participants, there will always be a number k between 50 and 100 such that k% is taken by% of the participants.

a. Minimum wage law
b. Pareto principle
c. Competition law
d. Beneficial ownership

16. _____ is the process of understanding, anticipating and influencing consumer behavior in order to maximize revenue or profits from a fixed, perishable resource This process was first discovered by Dr. Matt H. Keller. The challenge is to sell the right resources to the right customer at the right time for the right price.

a. Coopetition
b. Subscription
c. Freebie marketing
d. Yield management

Chapter 7. Quality Management and the Toyota Production System 33

17. A _____ is:

- Rewrite _____, in generative grammar and computer science
- Standardization, a formal and widely-accepted statement, fact, definition, or qualification
- Operation, a determinate _____ for performing a mathematical operation and obtaining a certain result (Mathematics, Logic)
    - Unary operation
    - Binary operation
- _____ of inference, a function from sets of formulae to formulae (Mathematics, Logic)
- _____ of thumb, principle with broad application that is not intended to be strictly accurate or reliable for every situation. Also often simply referred to as a _____
- Moral, an atomic element of a moral code for guiding choices in human behavior
- Heuristic, a quantized '_____' which shows a tendency or probability for successful function
- A regulation, as in sports
- A Production _____, as in computer science
- Procedural law, a _____ set governing the application of laws to cases
    - A law, which may informally be called a '_____'
    - A court ruling, a decision by a court
- In the U.S. Government, a regulation mandated by Congress, but written or expanded upon by the Executive Branch.
- Norm (sociology), an informal but widely accepted _____, concept, truth, definition, or qualification (social norms, legal norms, coding norms)
- Norm (philosophy), a kind of sentence or a reason to act, feel or believe
- 'Rulership' is the concept of governance by a government:
    - Military _____, governance by a military body
    - Monastic _____, a collection of precepts that guides the life of monks or nuns in a religious order where the superior holds the place of Christ
- Slide _____

- '_____,' a song by Ayumi Hamasaki
- '_____,' a song by rapper Nas
- '_____s,' an album by the band The Whitest Boy Alive
- _____s: Pyaar Ka Superhit Formula, a 2003 Bollywood film
- ruler, an instrument for measuring lengths
- _____, a component of an astrolabe, circumferator or similar instrument
- The _____s, a bestselling self-help book
- _____ Project (Run Up-to-date Linux Everywhere), a project that aims to use up-to-date Linux software on old PCs
- _____ engine, a software system that helps managing business _____s
- Ja _____, a hip hop artist
    - R.U.L.E., a 2005 greatest hits album by rapper Ja _____
- '_____s,' a KMFDM song

Chapter 7. Quality Management and the Toyota Production System

a. Demand
b. Procter ' Gamble
c. Technocracy
d. Rule

18. _____, or a _____ is the concept of a resulting effect (cf. cause and effect, arising from another action. In general terms, it is used to indicate that all human actions, particularly crime and sin, have profound effects.
    a. Solved
    b. Rule
    c. Variability
    d. Consequence

19. Autonomation describes a feature of machine design to effect the principle of _____ used in the Toyota Production System (TPS) and Lean manufacturing. It may be described as 'intelligent automation' or 'automation with a human touch.' This type of automation implements some supervisory functions rather than production functions. At Toyota this usually means that if an abnormal situation arises the machine stops and the worker will stop the production line.
    a. Vendor lock-in
    b. Jidoka
    c. Discrete manufacturing
    d. Flexible manufacturing

20. _____ is a Japanese philosophy that focuses on continuous improvement throughout all aspects of life. When applied to the workplace, _____ activities continually improve all functions of a business, from manufacturing to management and from the CEO to the assembly line workers. By improving standardized activities and processes, _____ aims to eliminate waste .
    a. Forfaiting
    b. Business failure
    c. Product life cycle
    d. Kaizen

21. '_____' is Step 7 of 'Philip Crosby's 14 Step Quality Improvement Process' . Although applicable to any type of enterprise, it has been primarily adopted within industry supply chains wherever large volumes of components are being purchased (common items such as nuts and bolts are good examples.)

_____ was a quality control program originated by the Denver Division of the Martin Marietta Corporation (now Lockheed Martin) on the Titan Missile program, which carried the first astronauts into space in the late 1960s.

a. 1921 recession
b. 100-year flood
c. Zero defects
d. 130-30 fund

22. A _____ is a volunteer group composed of workers (or even students), usually under the leadership of their supervisor (but they can elect a team leader), who are trained to identify, analyse and solve work-related problems and present their solutions to management in order to improve the performance of the organization, and motivate and enrich the work of employees. When matured, true _____s become self-managing, having gained the confidence of management. _____s are an alternative to the dehumanising concept of the Division of Labour, where workers or individuals are treated like robots.
a. De minimis fringe benefits
b. Consumption
c. Developed markets
d. Quality circle

Chapter 8. Betting on Uncertain Demand: The Newsvendor Model

1. Economics:

   - _____, the desire to own something and the ability to pay for it
   - _____ curve, a graphic representation of a _____ schedule
   - _____ deposit, the money in checking accounts
   - _____ pull theory, the theory that inflation occurs when _____ for goods and services exceeds existing supplies
   - _____ schedule, a table that lists the quantity of a good a person will buy it each different price
   - _____ side economics, the school of economics at believes government spending and tax cuts open economy by raising _____

   a. McKesson ' Robbins scandal
   b. Production
   c. Variability
   d. Demand

2. In microeconomics, _____ is quite simply the conversion of inputs into outputs. It is an economic process that uses resources to create a good or service that is suitable for exchange. This can include manufacturing, storing, shipping, and packaging.
   a. Production
   b. MET
   c. Solved
   d. Red Guards

3. _____s is the social science that studies the production, distribution, and consumption of goods and services. The term _____s comes from the Ancient Greek oá¼°κονομῖα from oá¼¶κος (oikos, 'house') + vÏŒμος (nomos, 'custom' or 'law'), hence 'rules of the house(hold)'. Current _____ models developed out of the broader field of political economy in the late 19th century, owing to a desire to use an empirical approach more akin to the physical sciences.
   a. Economic
   b. Inflation
   c. Energy economics
   d. Opportunity cost

4. _____ is the level of inventory that minimizes the total inventory holding costs and ordering costs. The framework used to determine this order quantity is also known as Wilson _____ Model. The model was developed by F. W. Harris in 1913.

a. Economic order quantity
b. AD-IA Model
c. ACEA agreement
d. ACCRA Cost of Living Index

5. In economics, _____ are business expenses that are not dependent on the activities of the business They tend to be time-related, such as salaries or rents being paid per month. This is in contrast to variable costs, which are volume-related (and are paid per quantity.)

In management accounting, _____ are defined as expenses that do not change in proportion to the activity of a business, within the relevant period or scale of production.

a. Quality costs
b. Cost-Volume-Profit Analysis
c. Fixed costs
d. Cost of poor quality

6. _____ means random.

A _____ process is one whose behavior is non-deterministic in that a system's subsequent state is determined both by the process's predictable actions and by a random element. _____ crafts are complex systems whose practitioners, even if complete experts, acknowledge that outcomes result from both known and unknown causes.

a. 130-30 fund
b. Stochastic
c. 100-year flood
d. Theory

7. _____ is the activity of estimating the quantity of a product or service that consumers will purchase. _____ involves techniques including both informal methods, such as educated guesses, and quantitative methods, such as the use of historical sales data or current data from test markets. _____ may be used in making pricing decisions, in assessing future capacity requirements, or in making decisions on whether to enter a new market.

a. Cost price
b. Financial Reporting
c. Finance designations
d. Demand forecasting

Chapter 8. Betting on Uncertain Demand: The Newsvendor Model

8. _____ is the process of estimation in unknown situations. Prediction is a similar, but more general term. Both can refer to estimation of time series, cross-sectional or longitudinal data.
   a. 130-30 fund
   b. 1921 recession
   c. 100-year flood
   d. Forecasting

9. Straight-line depreciation is the simplest and most-often-used technique, in which the company estimates the _____ of the asset at the end of the period during which it will be used to generate revenues (useful life) and will expense a portion of original cost in equal increments over that period. The _____ is an estimate of the value of the asset at the time it will be sold or disposed of; it may be zero or even negative. _____ is also known as scrap value or residual value.
   a. Depreciation
   b. Historical cost
   c. Fixed investment
   d. Salvage value

10. _____ is the a method of technical and economic research of the systems for purpose to optimize a parity between system's consumer functions or properties and expenses to achieve those functions or properties.

This methodology for continuous perfection of production, industrial technologies, organizational structures was developed by Juryj Sobolev in 1948 at the 'Perm telephone factory'

- 1948 Juryj Sobolev - the first success in application of a method analysis at the 'Perm telephone factory' .
- 1949 - the first application for the invention as result of use of the new method.

Today in economically developed countries practically each enterprise or the company use methodology of the kind of functional-cost analysis as a practice of the quality management, most full satisfying to principles of standards of series ISO 9000.

- Interest of consumer not in products itself, but the advantage which it will receive from its usage.
- The consumer aspires to reduce his expenses
- Functions needed by consumer can be executed in the various ways, and, hence, with various efficiency and expenses. Among possible alternatives of realization of functions exist such in which the parity of quality and the price is the optimal for the consumer.

The goal of _____ is achievement of the highest consumer satisfaction of production at simultaneous decrease in all kinds of industrial expenses Classical _____ has three English synonyms - Value Engineering, Value Management, Value Analysis.

Chapter 8. Betting on Uncertain Demand: The Newsvendor Model

a. Willingness to pay
b. Function cost analysis
c. Monopoly wage
d. Staple financing

11. In molecular kinetic theory in physics, a particle's _____ is a function of seven variables, $f(x,y,z,t;v_x,v_y,v_z)$, which gives the number of particles per unit volume in phase space. It is the number of particles having approximately the velocity (v_x,v_y,v_z) near the place (x,y,z) and time (t). The usual normalization of the _____ is

$$n(x,y,z,t) = \int f\, dv_x\, dv_y\, dv_z$$

$$N(t) = \int n\, dx\, dy\, dz$$

Here, N is the total number of particles and n is the number density of particles - the number of particles per unit volume, or the density divided by the mass of individual particles.

a. 100-year flood
b. Distribution function
c. 130-30 fund
d. 1921 recession

12. In probability theory and statistics, the _____ is a discrete probability distribution that expresses the probability of a number of events occurring in a fixed period of time if these events occur with a known average rate and independently of the time since the last event. The _____ can also be used for the number of events in other specified intervals such as distance, area or volume.

The distribution was discovered by Siméon-Denis Poisson and published, together with his probability theory, in 1838 in his work Recherches sur la probabilité des jugements en matières criminelles et matière civile ('Research on the Probability of Judgments in Criminal and Civil Matters'.)

a. 100-year flood
b. Poisson distribution
c. 1921 recession
d. 130-30 fund

13. In statistics, an _____ is a cumulative probability distribution function that concentrates probability 1/n at each of the n numbers in a sample.

Let $X_1, \ldots, X_n$ be iid real random variables with the cdf $F(x)$. The _____ $\hat{F}_n(x)$ is a step function defined by

$$\hat{F}_n(x) = \frac{\text{number of elements in the sample} \leq x}{n} = \frac{1}{n}\sum_{i=1}^{n} I(X_i \leq x),$$

where $I(A)$ is the indicator of event A.

a. Empirical distribution function
b. AD-IA Model
c. ACCRA Cost of Living Index
d. ACEA agreement

14. In probability theory and statistics, the _____ or Gaussian distribution is a continuous probability distribution that describes data that clusters around a mean or average. The graph of the associated probability density function is bell-shaped, with a peak at the mean, and is known as the Gaussian function or bell curve.

The _____ can be used to describe, at least approximately, any variable that tends to cluster around the mean.

a. 1921 recession
b. 100-year flood
c. Normal distribution
d. 130-30 fund

15. which is known as the _____ distribution. When properly scaled and translated, the corresponding cumulative distribution function is known as the error function.

The Gaussian distribution is named for Carl Friedrich Gauss, who used it to analyze astronomical data, and defined the formula for its probability density function.

a. 1921 recession
b. 100-year flood
c. 130-30 fund
d. Standard Normal

16. which is known as the _____. When properly scaled and translated, the corresponding cumulative distribution function is known as the error function.

The Gaussian distribution is named for Carl Friedrich Gauss, who used it to analyze astronomical data, and defined the formula for its probability density function.

   a. 130-30 fund
   b. 1921 recession
   c. 100-year flood
   d. Standard Normal Distribution

17. In probability theory and statistics, _____ is a measure of the variability or dispersion of a population, a data set, or a probability distribution. A low _____ indicates that the data points tend to be very close to the same value (the mean), while high _____ indicates that the data are 'spread out' over a large range of values.

For example, the average height for adult men in the United States is about 70 inches, with a _____ of around 3 inches.

   a. Standard deviation
   b. 1921 recession
   c. 130-30 fund
   d. 100-year flood

18. In probability and statistics the _____ distribution (including the Pascal distribution or Polya distribution) is a discrete probability distribution. It arises as the probability distribution of the number of failures in a sequence of Bernoulli trials needed to get a specified (non-random) number of successes. If one throws a die repeatedly until the third time a '1' appears, then the probability distribution of the number of non-'1's that appear before the third '1' is a _____ distribution.
   a. 1921 recession
   b. 100-year flood
   c. 130-30 fund
   d. Negative binomial

19. _____ is the process of understanding, anticipating and influencing consumer behavior in order to maximize revenue or profits from a fixed, perishable resource This process was first discovered by Dr. Matt H. Keller. The challenge is to sell the right resources to the right customer at the right time for the right price.

a. Subscription
b. Coopetition
c. Freebie marketing
d. Yield management

20. A _____ is an expression that compares quantities relative to each other. The most common examples involve two quantities, but any number of quantities can be compared. _____s are represented mathematically by separating each quantity with a colon, for example the _____ 2:3, which is read as the _____ 'two to three'.
a. 100-year flood
b. Y-intercept
c. 130-30 fund
d. Ratio

Chapter 8. Betting on Uncertain Demand: The Newsvendor Model   43

21. A _____ is:

- Rewrite _____, in generative grammar and computer science
- Standardization, a formal and widely-accepted statement, fact, definition, or qualification
- Operation, a determinate _____ for performing a mathematical operation and obtaining a certain result (Mathematics, Logic)
    - Unary operation
    - Binary operation
- _____ of inference, a function from sets of formulae to formulae (Mathematics, Logic)
- _____ of thumb, principle with broad application that is not intended to be strictly accurate or reliable for every situation. Also often simply referred to as a _____
- Moral, an atomic element of a moral code for guiding choices in human behavior
- Heuristic, a quantized '_____' which shows a tendency or probability for successful function
- A regulation, as in sports
- A Production _____, as in computer science
- Procedural law, a _____ set governing the application of laws to cases
    - A law, which may informally be called a '_____'
    - A court ruling, a decision by a court
- In the U.S. Government, a regulation mandated by Congress, but written or expanded upon by the Executive Branch.
- Norm (sociology), an informal but widely accepted _____, concept, truth, definition, or qualification (social norms, legal norms, coding norms)
- Norm (philosophy), a kind of sentence or a reason to act, feel or believe
- 'Rulership' is the concept of governance by a government:
    - Military _____, governance by a military body
    - Monastic _____, a collection of precepts that guides the life of monks or nuns in a religious order where the superior holds the place of Christ
- Slide _____

- '_____,' a song by Ayumi Hamasaki
- '_____,' a song by rapper Nas
- '_____s,' an album by the band The Whitest Boy Alive
- _____s: Pyaar Ka Superhit Formula, a 2003 Bollywood film
- ruler, an instrument for measuring lengths
- _____, a component of an astrolabe, circumferator or similar instrument
- The _____s, a bestselling self-help book
- _____ Project (Run Up-to-date Linux Everywhere), a project that aims to use up-to-date Linux software on old PCs
- _____ engine, a software system that helps managing business _____s
- Ja _____, a hip hop artist
    - R.U.L.E., a 2005 greatest hits album by rapper Ja _____
- '_____s,' a KMFDM song

a. Rule
b. Demand
c. Procter ' Gamble
d. Technocracy

22. In statistics, decision theory and economics, a _____ is a function that maps an event (technically an element of a sample space) onto a real number representing the economic cost or regret associated with the event.

Less technically, in statistics a _____ represents the loss (cost in money or loss in utility in some other sense) associated with an estimate being 'wrong' (different from either a desired or a true value) as a function of a measure of the degree of wrongness (generally the difference between the estimated value and the true or desired value.)

Both Frequentist and Bayesian statistical theory involve calculating statistics in such a way as to minimize the expected loss observed from being wrong given a set of assumptions about the data and one's _____.

a. Population modeling
b. 100-year flood
c. Window function
d. Loss Function

23. _____ is a way of expressing knowledge or belief that an event will occur or has occurred. In mathematics the concept has been given an exact meaning in _____ theory, that is used extensively in such areas of study as mathematics, statistics, finance, gambling, science, and philosophy to draw conclusions about the likelihood of potential events and the underlying mechanics of complex systems.

The word _____ does not have a consistent direct definition.

a. Probability
b. 130-30 fund
c. 100-year flood
d. 1921 recession

Chapter 9. Assemble-to-Order, Make-to-Order, and Quick Response with Reactive Capacity

1. _____ is a broad label that refers to any individuals or households that use goods and services generated within the economy. The concept of a _____ is used in different contexts, so that the usage and significance of the term may vary.

Typically when business people and economists talk of _____s they are talking about person as _____, an aggregated commodity item with little individuality other than that expressed in the buy/not-buy decision.

 a. 1921 recession
 b. 100-year flood
 c. Consumer
 d. 130-30 fund

2. _____s is the social science that studies the production, distribution, and consumption of goods and services. The term _____s comes from the Ancient Greek oá¼°κονομῖα from oá¼¶κος (oikos, 'house') + vĪŒμος (nomos, 'custom' or 'law'), hence 'rules of the house(hold)'. Current _____ models developed out of the broader field of political economy in the late 19th century, owing to a desire to use an empirical approach more akin to the physical sciences.
 a. Inflation
 b. Opportunity cost
 c. Energy economics
 d. Economic

3. _____ is the level of inventory that minimizes the total inventory holding costs and ordering costs. The framework used to determine this order quantity is also known as Wilson _____ Model. The model was developed by F. W. Harris in 1913.
 a. AD-IA Model
 b. Economic order quantity
 c. ACEA agreement
 d. ACCRA Cost of Living Index

4. _____ is a joint trade and industry body working towards making the grocery sector as a whole more responsive to consumer demand and promote the removal of unnecessary costs from the supply chain.

The _____ movement beginning in the mid-nineties was characterized by the emergence of new principles of collaborative management along the supply chain. It was understood that companies can serve consumers better, faster and at less cost by working together with trading partners.

Chapter 9. Assemble-to-Order, Make-to-Order, and Quick Response with Reactive Capacity

   a. ACCRA Cost of Living Index
   b. ACEA agreement
   c. AD-IA Model
   d. Efficient Consumer Response

5. Economics:

   - _____, the desire to own something and the ability to pay for it
   - _____ curve, a graphic representation of a _____ schedule
   - _____ deposit, the money in checking accounts
   - _____ pull theory, the theory that inflation occurs when _____ for goods and services exceeds existing supplies
   - _____ schedule, a table that lists the quantity of a good a person will buy it each different price
   - _____ side economics, the school of economics at believes government spending and tax cuts open economy by raising _____

   a. Demand
   b. Production
   c. Variability
   d. McKesson ' Robbins scandal

6. _____ is the process of understanding, anticipating and influencing consumer behavior in order to maximize revenue or profits from a fixed, perishable resource This process was first discovered by Dr. Matt H. Keller. The challenge is to sell the right resources to the right customer at the right time for the right price.
   a. Coopetition
   b. Yield management
   c. Freebie marketing
   d. Subscription

7. A _____ is an expression that compares quantities relative to each other. The most common examples involve two quantities, but any number of quantities can be compared. _____s are represented mathematically by separating each quantity with a colon, for example the _____ 2:3, which is read as the _____ 'two to three'.
   a. 130-30 fund
   b. Y-intercept
   c. 100-year flood
   d. Ratio

Chapter 9. Assemble-to-Order, Make-to-Order, and Quick Response with Reactive Capacity

8. In molecular kinetic theory in physics, a particle's _____ is a function of seven variables, f(x,y,z,t;v$_x$,v$_y$,v$_z$), which gives the number of particles per unit volume in phase space. It is the number of particles having approximately the velocity (v$_x$,v$_y$,v$_z$) near the place (x,y,z) and time (t). The usual normalization of the _____ is

$$n(x, y, z, t) = \int f \, dv_x \, dv_y \, dv_z$$

$$N(t) = \int n \, dx \, dy \, dz$$

Here, N is the total number of particles and n is the number density of particles - the number of particles per unit volume, or the density divided by the mass of individual particles.

   a. 130-30 fund
   b. Distribution Function
   c. 100-year flood
   d. 1921 recession

9. In probability theory and statistics, the _____ or Gaussian distribution is a continuous probability distribution that describes data that clusters around a mean or average. The graph of the associated probability density function is bell-shaped, with a peak at the mean, and is known as the Gaussian function or bell curve.

The _____ can be used to describe, at least approximately, any variable that tends to cluster around the mean.

   a. Normal Distribution
   b. 100-year flood
   c. 1921 recession
   d. 130-30 fund

10. which is known as the _____ distribution. When properly scaled and translated, the corresponding cumulative distribution function is known as the error function.

The Gaussian distribution is named for Carl Friedrich Gauss, who used it to analyze astronomical data, and defined the formula for its probability density function.

a. 130-30 fund
b. 1921 recession
c. 100-year flood
d. Standard Normal

11. which is known as the _____. When properly scaled and translated, the corresponding cumulative distribution function is known as the error function.

The Gaussian distribution is named for Carl Friedrich Gauss, who used it to analyze astronomical data, and defined the formula for its probability density function.

a. Standard Normal Distribution
b. 1921 recession
c. 130-30 fund
d. 100-year flood

12. Necessary _____s:

If x is a necessary _____ of y, then the presence of y necessarily implies the presence of x. The presence of x, however, does not imply that y will occur.

Sufficient _____s:

If x is a sufficient _____ of y, then the presence of x necessarily implies the presence of y.

a. Philosophy of economics
b. Political philosophy
c. Materialism
d. Cause

13. In mathematics, a _____ is a constant multiplicative factor of a certain object. For example, in the expression $9x^2$, the _____ of x^2 is 9.

The object can be such things as a variable, a vector, a function, etc.

Chapter 9. Assemble-to-Order, Make-to-Order, and Quick Response with Reactive Capacity 49

a. 100-year flood
b. 130-30 fund
c. 1921 recession
d. Coefficient

14. The term _____, 'the state or characteristic of being variable', _____ describes how spread out or closely clustered a set of data is. may be applied to many different subjects:

- Climate _____
- Genetic _____
- Heart rate _____
- Human _____
- Solar van
- Spatial _____
- Statistical _____
- _____

a. Demand
b. Variability
c. Characteristic
d. Total product

15. In mathematics, a _____ system is a system which is not linear, that is, a system which does not satisfy the superposition principle, or whose output is not proportional to its input. Less technically, a _____ system is any problem where the variable(s) to be solved for cannot be written as a linear combination of independent components. A nonhomogeneous system, which is linear apart from the presence of a function of the independent variables, is _____ according to a strict definition, but such systems are usually studied alongside linear systems, because they can be transformed to a linear system of multiple variables.

a. 100-year flood
b. 130-30 fund
c. Nonlinear system
d. Nonlinear

16. _____ manufacturing is an operations strategy and is primarily designed and focused on the following four major items which are really the key to success.

Cost: low cost producer.

Quality: Quality is further divided in to two namely Product quality and Process quality.

Chapter 9. Assemble-to-Order, Make-to-Order, and Quick Response with Reactive Capacity

a. Quick Response
b. Private sector
c. Six sigma
d. Secondary sector of the economy

17. _____ is the state of being which occurs when a person, object, or service is no longer wanted even though it may still be in good working order. _____ frequently occurs because a replacement has become available that is superior in one or more aspects. Videotapes making way for DVDs

Technical _____ may occur when a new product or technology supersedes the old, and it becomes preferred to utilize the new technology in place of the old.

a. ACEA agreement
b. AD-IA Model
c. Obsolescence
d. ACCRA Cost of Living Index

18. _____, in marketing, manufacturing, call centres and management, is the use of flexible computer-aided manufacturing systems to produce custom output. Those systems combine the low unit costs of mass production processes with the flexibility of individual customization.

'_____' is the new frontier in business competition for both manufacturing and service industries.

a. 1921 recession
b. 130-30 fund
c. 100-year flood
d. Mass customization

19. In microeconomics, _____ is quite simply the conversion of inputs into outputs. It is an economic process that uses resources to create a good or service that is suitable for exchange. This can include manufacturing, storing, shipping, and packaging.
a. Solved
b. Red Guards
c. Production
d. MET

Chapter 10. Service Levels and Lead Times in Supply Chains: The Order-up-to Inventory Model

1. Economics:

    - _____, the desire to own something and the ability to pay for it
    - _____ curve, a graphic representation of a _____ schedule
    - _____ deposit, the money in checking accounts
    - _____ pull theory, the theory that inflation occurs when _____ for goods and services exceeds existing supplies
    - _____ schedule, a table that lists the quantity of a good a person will buy it each different price
    - _____ side economics, the school of economics at believes government spending and tax cuts open economy by raising _____

    a. Demand
    b. Variability
    c. McKesson ' Robbins scandal
    d. Production

2. A _____ is an object whose consumption increases the utility of the consumer, for which the quantity demanded exceeds the quantity supplied at zero price. _____s are usually modeled as having diminishing marginal utility. The first individual purchase has high utility; the second has less.
    a. Composite good
    b. Merit good
    c. Pie method
    d. Good

3. In microeconomics, _____ is quite simply the conversion of inputs into outputs. It is an economic process that uses resources to create a good or service that is suitable for exchange. This can include manufacturing, storing, shipping, and packaging.
    a. Production
    b. Red Guards
    c. Solved
    d. MET

4. _____ is a concept with somewhat disparate meanings in several fields. It also has a common meaning which has a loose connection with some of those more definite meanings.

Casually, it is typically used to denote a lack of order, or purpose, or cause.

Chapter 10. Service Levels and Lead Times in Supply Chains: The Order-up-to Inventory Model

a. Randomness
b. 1921 recession
c. 130-30 fund
d. 100-year flood

5. _____ is the term denoting either an entrance or changes which are inserted into a system and which activate/modify a process. It is an abstract concept, used in the modeling, system(s) design and system(s) exploitation. It is usually connected with other terms, e.g., _____ field, _____ variable, _____ parameter, _____ value, _____ signal, _____ device and _____ file.
a. ACEA agreement
b. AD-IA Model
c. Input
d. ACCRA Cost of Living Index

6. _____: A distribution term that refers to the status of items on a purchase order in the event that some or all of the inventory required to fulfill the order is insufficient to satisfy demand. This differs from a forward order where stock is available but delivery is postponed for another reason.

_____ Cost: A cost incurred by a business when it is unable to fill an order and must complete it later.

a. Poverty penalty
b. Teaser rate
c. Centralization
d. Backorder

7. A _____ is the period of time between the initiation of any process of production and the completion of that process. Thus the _____ for ordering a new car from a manufacturer may be anywhere from 2 weeks to 6 months. In industry, _____ reduction is an important part of lean manufacturing.
a. Lead time
b. 1921 recession
c. 100-year flood
d. 130-30 fund

8. _____ is the state of being which occurs when a person, object, or service is no longer wanted even though it may still be in good working order. _____ frequently occurs because a replacement has become available that is superior in one or more aspects. Videotapes making way for DVDs

Chapter 10. Service Levels and Lead Times in Supply Chains: The Order-up-to Inventory Model

Technical _____ may occur when a new product or technology supersedes the old, and it becomes preferred to utilize the new technology in place of the old.

a. ACCRA Cost of Living Index
b. AD-IA Model
c. ACEA agreement
d. Obsolescence

9. _____ is a concept related to lean and just-in-time (JIT) production. The Japanese word _____ is a common term meaning 'signboard' or 'billboard'. According to Taiichi Ohno, the man credited with developing JIT, _____ is a means through which JIT is achieved.

a. Kanban
b. Penny stock
c. Risk management
d. Non-disclosure agreement

10. _____ can be considered to have three main components: quality control, quality assurance and quality improvement. _____ is focused not only on product quality, but also the means to achieve it. _____ therefore uses quality assurance and control of processes as well as products to achieve more consistent quality.

a. 1921 recession
b. 100-year flood
c. 130-30 fund
d. Quality management

11. _____ is a way of expressing knowledge or belief that an event will occur or has occurred. In mathematics the concept has been given an exact meaning in _____ theory, that is used extensively in such areas of study as mathematics, statistics, finance, gambling, science, and philosophy to draw conclusions about the likelihood of potential events and the underlying mechanics of complex systems.

The word _____ does not have a consistent direct definition.

a. 130-30 fund
b. 100-year flood
c. 1921 recession
d. Probability

Chapter 10. Service Levels and Lead Times in Supply Chains: The Order-up-to Inventory Model

12. In statistics, many time series exhibit cyclic variation known as _____, periodic variation, or periodic fluctuations. This variation can be either regular or semiregular.

For example, retail sales tend to peak for the Christmas season and then decline after the holidays.

   a. Linear prediction
   b. Trispectrum
   c. Seasonal adjustment
   d. Seasonality

13. In probability theory and statistics, _____ is a measure of the variability or dispersion of a population, a data set, or a probability distribution. A low _____ indicates that the data points tend to be very close to the same value (the mean), while high _____ indicates that the data are 'spread out' over a large range of values.

For example, the average height for adult men in the United States is about 70 inches, with a _____ of around 3 inches.

   a. 100-year flood
   b. 1921 recession
   c. Standard deviation
   d. 130-30 fund

14. In probability theory and statistics, the _____ or Gaussian distribution is a continuous probability distribution that describes data that clusters around a mean or average. The graph of the associated probability density function is bell-shaped, with a peak at the mean, and is known as the Gaussian function or bell curve.

The _____ can be used to describe, at least approximately, any variable that tends to cluster around the mean.

   a. 130-30 fund
   b. 100-year flood
   c. 1921 recession
   d. Normal distribution

15. In probability theory and statistics, the _____ is a discrete probability distribution that expresses the probability of a number of events occurring in a fixed period of time if these events occur with a known average rate and independently of the time since the last event. The _____ can also be used for the number of events in other specified intervals such as distance, area or volume.

Chapter 10. Service Levels and Lead Times in Supply Chains: The Order-up-to Inventory Model

The distribution was discovered by Siméon-Denis Poisson and published, together with his probability theory, in 1838 in his work Recherches sur la probabilité des jugements en matières criminelles et matière civile ('Research on the Probability of Judgments in Criminal and Civil Matters'.)

   a. 100-year flood
   b. 1921 recession
   c. Poisson distribution
   d. 130-30 fund

16. In statistics, decision theory and economics, a _____ is a function that maps an event (technically an element of a sample space) onto a real number representing the economic cost or regret associated with the event.

Less technically, in statistics a _____ represents the loss (cost in money or loss in utility in some other sense) associated with an estimate being 'wrong' (different from either a desired or a true value) as a function of a measure of the degree of wrongness (generally the difference between the estimated value and the true or desired value.)

Both Frequentist and Bayesian statistical theory involve calculating statistics in such a way as to minimize the expected loss observed from being wrong given a set of assumptions about the data and one's _____.

   a. Loss Function
   b. Window function
   c. Population modeling
   d. 100-year flood

17. _____, or a _____ is the concept of a resulting effect (cf. cause and effect, arising from another action. In general terms, it is used to indicate that all human actions, particularly crime and sin, have profound effects.
   a. Solved
   b. Variability
   c. Rule
   d. Consequence

18. which is known as the _____ distribution. When properly scaled and translated, the corresponding cumulative distribution function is known as the error function.

The Gaussian distribution is named for Carl Friedrich Gauss, who used it to analyze astronomical data, and defined the formula for its probability density function.

Chapter 10. Service Levels and Lead Times in Supply Chains: The Order-up-to Inventory Model

a. Standard Normal
b. 1921 recession
c. 100-year flood
d. 130-30 fund

19. which is known as the _____. When properly scaled and translated, the corresponding cumulative distribution function is known as the error function.

The Gaussian distribution is named for Carl Friedrich Gauss, who used it to analyze astronomical data, and defined the formula for its probability density function.

a. Standard Normal Distribution
b. 130-30 fund
c. 100-year flood
d. 1921 recession

20. _____s is the social science that studies the production, distribution, and consumption of goods and services. The term _____s comes from the Ancient Greek oá¼°κονομῖα from oá¼¶κος (oikos, 'house') + vÏŒμος (nomos, 'custom' or 'law'), hence 'rules of the house(hold)'. Current _____ models developed out of the broader field of political economy in the late 19th century, owing to a desire to use an empirical approach more akin to the physical sciences.
a. Energy economics
b. Economic
c. Inflation
d. Opportunity cost

21. _____ is the level of inventory that minimizes the total inventory holding costs and ordering costs. The framework used to determine this order quantity is also known as Wilson _____ Model. The model was developed by F. W. Harris in 1913.
a. ACCRA Cost of Living Index
b. Economic order quantity
c. AD-IA Model
d. ACEA agreement

22. In economics, _____ are business expenses that are not dependent on the activities of the business They tend to be time-related, such as salaries or rents being paid per month. This is in contrast to variable costs, which are volume-related (and are paid per quantity.)

Chapter 10. Service Levels and Lead Times in Supply Chains: The Order-up-to Inventory Model

In management accounting, _____ are defined as expenses that do not change in proportion to the activity of a business, within the relevant period or scale of production.

a. Cost-Volume-Profit Analysis
b. Quality costs
c. Cost of poor quality
d. Fixed costs

23. _____ Management is the succession of strategies used by management as a product goes through its _____. The conditions in which a product is sold changes over time and must be managed as it moves through its succession of stages.

The _____ goes through many phases, involves many professional disciplines, and requires many skills, tools and processes.

a. Product life cycle
b. Procurement
c. Tax profit
d. Corporate tax

24. In statistics the _____ of an event i is the number n_i of times the event occurred in the experiment or the study. These frequencies are often graphically represented in histograms.

We speak of absolute frequencies, when the counts n_i themselves are given and of (relative) frequencies, when those are normalized by the total number of events:

$$f_i = \frac{n_i}{N} = \frac{n_i}{\sum_i n_i}.$$

Taking the f_i for all i and tabulating or plotting them leads to a _____ distribution.

a. 1921 recession
b. 130-30 fund
c. 100-year flood
d. Frequency

25. In business management, _____ often referred to as stockturn, stock turns, turns, and stock turnover.

Chapter 10. Service Levels and Lead Times in Supply Chains: The Order-up-to Inventory Model

This measures the number of times invested in goods to be sold or used over in a year.

$$\text{Inventory Turns} = \frac{Cost of Goods Sold (over a given period)}{Average Inventory (for the period)}$$

An item whose inventory is sold (turns over) once a year has higher holding cost than one that turns over twice, or three times, or more in that time.

a. AD-IA Model
b. ACCRA Cost of Living Index
c. Inventory turns
d. ACEA agreement

26. _____ is a practice in logistics of unloading materials from an incoming semi-trailer truck or rail car and loading these materials directly into outbound trucks, trailers with little or no storage in between. This may be done to change type of conveyance, to sort material intended for different destinations or similar destination.

Cross-Dock operations were first pioneered in the US trucking industry in the 1930's, and have been in continuous use in LTL (less than truckload) operations ever since.

a. Business process automation
b. Long squeeze
c. Business development
d. Cross-docking

Chapter 11. Risk-Pooling Strategies to Reduce and Hedge Uncertainty

1. Economics:

    - _____, the desire to own something and the ability to pay for it
    - _____ curve, a graphic representation of a _____ schedule
    - _____ deposit, the money in checking accounts
    - _____ pull theory, the theory that inflation occurs when _____ for goods and services exceeds existing supplies
    - _____ schedule, a table that lists the quantity of a good a person will buy it each different price
    - _____ side economics, the school of economics at believes government spending and tax cuts open economy by raising _____

    a. Variability
    b. Demand
    c. Production
    d. McKesson ' Robbins scandal

2. In probability theory and statistics, the _____ is a discrete probability distribution that expresses the probability of a number of events occurring in a fixed period of time if these events occur with a known average rate and independently of the time since the last event. The _____ can also be used for the number of events in other specified intervals such as distance, area or volume.

    The distribution was discovered by Siméon-Denis Poisson and published, together with his probability theory, in 1838 in his work Recherches sur la probabilité des jugements en matières criminelles et matière civile ('Research on the Probability of Judgments in Criminal and Civil Matters'.)

    a. 1921 recession
    b. 130-30 fund
    c. 100-year flood
    d. Poisson distribution

3. In probability theory and statistics, _____ is a measure of the variability or dispersion of a population, a data set, or a probability distribution. A low _____ indicates that the data points tend to be very close to the same value (the mean), while high _____ indicates that the data are 'spread out' over a large range of values.

    For example, the average height for adult men in the United States is about 70 inches, with a _____ of around 3 inches.

a. 130-30 fund
b. 1921 recession
c. 100-year flood
d. Standard deviation

4. _____, or a _____ is the concept of a resulting effect (cf. cause and effect, arising from another action. In general terms, it is used to indicate that all human actions, particularly crime and sin, have profound effects.
   a. Variability
   b. Solved
   c. Consequence
   d. Rule

5. An _____ is a retailer that primarily uses the Internet as a medium for customers to shop for the goods or services provided.

The word _____ is a portmanteau word derived from 'electronic' and 'retailer', in a similar way to 'e-mail'. The word has been in use since at least 1995.

   a. Electronic commerce
   b. Electronic Data Interchange
   c. E-tailer
   d. Automated Clearing House

6. _____, commonly known as (electronic marketing) e-commerce or eCommerce, consists of the buying and selling of products or services over electronic systems such as the Internet and other computer networks. The amount of trade conducted electronically has grown extraordinarily with widespread Internet usage. The use of commerce is conducted in this way, spurring and drawing on innovations in electronic funds transfer, supply chain management, Internet marketing, online transaction processing, electronic data interchange (EDI), inventory management systems, and automated data collection systems.
   a. Automated Clearing House
   b. Auction software
   c. Electronic Data Interchange
   d. Electronic commerce

7. _____ is a supply chain management technique in which the retailer does not keep goods in stock, but instead transfers customer orders and shipment details to either the manufacturer or a wholesaler, who then ships the goods directly to the customer. As in all retail businesses, the retailers make their profit on the difference between the wholesale and retail price.

Some _____ retailers may keep 'show' items on display in stores, so that customers can inspect an item similar to those that they can purchase.

a. Drop shipping
b. 130-30 fund
c. 100-year flood
d. Purchasing

8. _____ is a relatively new paradigm that emerged from 'barrier-free' or 'accessible design' and 'assistive technology.' _____ strives to be a broad-spectrum solution that produces buildings, products and environments that are usable and effective for everyone, not just people with disabilities. Moreover, it recognizes the importance of how things look. For example, while built up handles are a way to make utensils more usable for people with gripping limitations, some companies introduced larger, easy to grip and attractive handles as feature of mass produced utensils.

a. AD-IA Model
b. ACEA agreement
c. Universal design
d. ACCRA Cost of Living Index

9. In mathematics, a _____ is a constant multiplicative factor of a certain object. For example, in the expression $9x^2$, the _____ of x^2 is 9.

The object can be such things as a variable, a vector, a function, etc.

a. Coefficient
b. 1921 recession
c. 100-year flood
d. 130-30 fund

10. In statistics, _____ indicates the strength and direction of a linear relationship between two random variables. That is in contrast with the usage of the term in colloquial speech, which denotes any relationship, not necessarily linear. In general statistical usage, _____ or co-relation refers to the departure of two random variables from independence.

a. 1921 recession
b. 130-30 fund
c. 100-year flood
d. Correlation

Chapter 11. Risk-Pooling Strategies to Reduce and Hedge Uncertainty

11. _____ is a concept with somewhat disparate meanings in several fields. It also has a common meaning which has a loose connection with some of those more definite meanings.

Casually, it is typically used to denote a lack of order, or purpose, or cause.

a. 1921 recession
b. 130-30 fund
c. 100-year flood
d. Randomness

12. _____, in microeconomics, are the cost advantages that a business obtains due to expansion. They are factors that cause a producere;s average cost per unit to fall as scale is increased. _____ is a long run concept and refers to reductions in unit cost as the size of a facility, or scale, increases.

a. Isoquant
b. Economic production quantity
c. Underinvestment employment relationship
d. Economies of scale

13. A _____ is the period of time between the initiation of any process of production and the completion of that process. Thus the _____ for ordering a new car from a manufacturer may be anywhere from 2 weeks to 6 months. In industry, _____ reduction is an important part of lean manufacturing.

a. 100-year flood
b. 1921 recession
c. Lead time
d. 130-30 fund

14. _____ occurs when organizations market many variations of the same products. This can be done through different colour combinations, product sizes and different product uses. This produces diversity for the firm as it is able to capture its sizeable portion of the market.

a. Price signal
b. Mohring effect
c. Marginal rate of technical substitution
d. Product proliferation

15. In molecular kinetic theory in physics, a particle's _____ is a function of seven variables, $f(x,y,z,t;v_x,v_y,v_z)$, which gives the number of particles per unit volume in phase space. It is the number of particles having approximately the velocity (v_x,v_y,v_z) near the place (x,y,z) and time (t). The usual normalization of the _____ is

Chapter 11. Risk-Pooling Strategies to Reduce and Hedge Uncertainty

$$n(x, y, z, t) = \int f \, dv_x \, dv_y \, dv_z$$

$$N(t) = \int n \, dx \, dy \, dz$$

Here, N is the total number of particles and n is the number density of particles - the number of particles per unit volume, or the density divided by the mass of individual particles.

a. 100-year flood
b. 130-30 fund
c. 1921 recession
d. Distribution Function

16. In statistics, decision theory and economics, a _____ is a function that maps an event (technically an element of a sample space) onto a real number representing the economic cost or regret associated with the event.

Less technically, in statistics a _____ represents the loss (cost in money or loss in utility in some other sense) associated with an estimate being 'wrong' (different from either a desired or a true value) as a function of a measure of the degree of wrongness (generally the difference between the estimated value and the true or desired value.)

Both Frequentist and Bayesian statistical theory involve calculating statistics in such a way as to minimize the expected loss observed from being wrong given a set of assumptions about the data and one's _____.

a. 100-year flood
b. Loss Function
c. Window function
d. Population modeling

17. _____ or Postponement is a concept in supply chain management where the manufacturing process starts by making a generic or family product that is later differentiated into a specific end-product. This is a widely used method, especially in industries with high demand uncertainty, and can be effectively used to address the final demand even if forecasts cannot be improved.

An example would be Benetton and their knitted sweaters that are initially all white, and then dyed into different colors only when the season/customer color preference/demand is known.

a. Demand side
b. Delayed differentiation
c. Vendor Managed Inventory
d. CPFR

18. A _____ is a place of residence or refuge and comfort. It is usually a place in which an individual or a family can rest and be able to store personal property. Most modern-day households contain sanitary facilities and a means of preparing food.
    a. 130-30 fund
    b. Home
    c. 1921 recession
    d. 100-year flood

19. A _____ system (_____S) is a manufacturing system in which there is some amount of flexibility that allows the system to react in the case of changes, whether predicted or unpredicted. This flexibility is generally considered to fall into two categories, which both contain numerous subcategories.

The first category, machine flexibility, covers the system's ability to be changed to produce new product types, and ability to change the order of operations executed on a part.

   a. Homeworkers
   b. Discrete manufacturing
   c. Flexible manufacturing
   d. Vendor lock-in

20. _____ was the American founder of the Ford Motor Company and father of modern assembly lines used in mass production. His introduction of the Model T automobile revolutionized transportation and American industry. He was a prolific inventor and was awarded 161 U.S. patents.
    a. Maximilian Carl Emil Weber
    b. George Cabot Lodge II
    c. Werner Sombart
    d. Henry Ford

21. _____ is a concept in economics which refers to the extent to which an enterprise or a nation actually uses its installed productive capacity. Thus, it refers to the relationship between actual output that 'is' produced with the installed equipment and the potential output which 'could' be produced with it, if capacity was fully used.

If market demand grows, _____ will rise.

Chapter 11. Risk-Pooling Strategies to Reduce and Hedge Uncertainty

a. Marginal product of labor
b. Long-run
c. Diseconomies of scale
d. Capacity utilization

22. _____ is an instructional procedure used in Behavioral psychology, experimental analysis of behavior and applied behavior analysis. It involves reinforcing individual responses occurring in a sequence to form a complex behavior. It is frequently used for training behavioral sequences (or 'chains') that are beyond the current repertoire of the learner.
   a. 130-30 fund
   b. 1921 recession
   c. 100-year flood
   d. Chaining

23. A contract manufacturer ('_____') is a firm that manufactures components or products for another 'hiring' firm. Many industries utilize this process, especially the aerospace, defense, computer, semiconductor, energy, medical, food manufacturing, personal care, and automotive fields. Some types of _____ include CNC machining, complex assembly, aluminum die casting, grinding, broaching, gears, and forging.
   a. Production-possibility frontier
   b. Marginal rate of transformation
   c. Contract manufacturing
   d. Piece work

Chapter 12. Revenue Management with Capacity Controls

1. _____ is the process of understanding, anticipating and influencing consumer behavior in order to maximize revenue or profits from a fixed, perishable resource This process was first discovered by Dr. Matt H. Keller. The challenge is to sell the right resources to the right customer at the right time for the right price.
    a. Coopetition
    b. Subscription
    c. Freebie marketing
    d. Yield management

2. _____s are expenses that change in proportion to the activity of a business. In other words, _____ is the sum of marginal costs. It can also be considered normal costs.
    a. Cost allocation
    b. Quality costs
    c. Cost-Volume-Profit Analysis
    d. Variable cost

3. In probability theory and statistics, the _____ is a discrete probability distribution that expresses the probability of a number of events occurring in a fixed period of time if these events occur with a known average rate and independently of the time since the last event. The _____ can also be used for the number of events in other specified intervals such as distance, area or volume.

    The distribution was discovered by Siméon-Denis Poisson and published, together with his probability theory, in 1838 in his work Recherches sur la probabilité des jugements en matières criminelles et matière civile ('Research on the Probability of Judgments in Criminal and Civil Matters'.)

    a. Poisson distribution
    b. 100-year flood
    c. 1921 recession
    d. 130-30 fund

4. A _____ is an expression that compares quantities relative to each other. The most common examples involve two quantities, but any number of quantities can be compared. _____s are represented mathematically by separating each quantity with a colon, for example the _____ 2:3, which is read as the _____ 'two to three'.
    a. 130-30 fund
    b. Y-intercept
    c. 100-year flood
    d. Ratio

5. _____ is a term used to describe the sale of access to a service which exceeds the capacity of the service.

Chapter 12. Revenue Management with Capacity Controls

In the telecommunications industry, _____ -- such as in the frame relay world -- means that a telephone company has sold access to too many customers which basically flood the telephone company's lines, resulting in an inability for some customers to use what they purchased.

Nevertheless this only happens when all users try to use the service at the same time and since nearly half of the users will not use the service at the same moment this almost never happens.

   a. ACEA agreement
   b. AD-IA Model
   c. ACCRA Cost of Living Index
   d. Overbooking

6. The _____ captures an expanded spectrum of values and criteria for measuring organizational (and societal) success: economic, ecological and social. With the ratification of the United Nations and ICLEI _____ standard for urban and community accounting in early 2007, this became the dominant approach to public sector full cost accounting. Similar UN standards apply to natural capital and human capital measurement to assist in measurements required by _____, e.g. the ecoBudget standard for reporting ecological footprint.
   a. Missing market
   b. Leapfrogging
   c. Social welfare function
   d. Triple bottom line

7. Economics:

   - _____ ,the desire to own something and the ability to pay for it
   - _____ curve,a graphic representation of a _____ schedule
   - _____ deposit, the money in checking accounts
   - _____ pull theory,the theory that inflation occurs when _____ for goods and services exceeds existing supplies
   - _____ schedule,a table that lists the quantity of a good a person will buy it each different price
   - _____ side economics,the school of economics at believes government spending and tax cuts open economy by raising _____

   a. McKesson ' Robbins scandal
   b. Production
   c. Variability
   d. Demand

Chapter 12. Revenue Management with Capacity Controls

8. _____ is the activity of estimating the quantity of a product or service that consumers will purchase. _____ involves techniques including both informal methods, such as educated guesses, and quantitative methods, such as the use of historical sales data or current data from test markets. _____ may be used in making pricing decisions, in assessing future capacity requirements, or in making decisions on whether to enter a new market.
   a. Demand forecasting
   b. Finance designations
   c. Financial Reporting
   d. Cost price

9. _____ is the process of estimation in unknown situations. Prediction is a similar, but more general term. Both can refer to estimation of time series, cross-sectional or longitudinal data.
   a. 1921 recession
   b. 100-year flood
   c. Forecasting
   d. 130-30 fund

10. _____ is one of the four Ps of the marketing mix. The other three aspects are product, promotion, and place. It is also a key variable in microeconomic price allocation theory.
   a. Pricing
   b. Guaranteed Maximum Price
   c. Point of total assumption
   d. Premium pricing

Chapter 13. Supply Chain Coordination

1. In economics and sociology, an _____ is any factor (financial or non-financial) that enables or motivates a particular course of action, or counts as a reason for preferring one choice to the alternatives. It is an expectation that encourages people to behave in a certain way. Since human beings are purposeful creatures, the study of _____ structures is central to the study of all economic activity (both in terms of individual decision-making and in terms of co-operation and competition within a larger institutional structure.)
    a. Isocost
    b. Epstein-Zin preferences
    c. Economic reform
    d. Incentive

2. _____ aims at improving supply chain performance by aligning the objectives of individual enterprises. It usually focuses on inventory management and ordering decisions in distributed settings. _____ models may involve multi-echelon inventory theory, multiple decision makers, asymmetric information, as well as recent paradigms of manufacturing, such as mass customization, short product life-cycles, outsourcing and delayed differentiation.
    a. Churn rate
    b. Next Eleven
    c. Big Business
    d. Channel coordination

3. Procter is a surname, and may also refer to:

    - Bryan Waller Procter (pseud. Barry Cornwall), English poet
    - Goodwin Procter, American law firm
    - _____, consumer products multinational

    a. Bucket shop
    b. Procter ' Gamble
    c. Drawdown
    d. Tightness

4. Necessary _____s:

If x is a necessary _____ of y, then the presence of y necessarily implies the presence of x. The presence of x, however, does not imply that y will occur.

Sufficient _____s:

If x is a sufficient _____ of y, then the presence of x necessarily implies the presence of y.

Chapter 13. Supply Chain Coordination

   a. Political philosophy
   b. Materialism
   c. Philosophy of economics
   d. Cause

5. _____, or a _____ is the concept of a resulting effect (cf. cause and effect, arising from another action. In general terms, it is used to indicate that all human actions, particularly crime and sin, have profound effects.
   a. Consequence
   b. Rule
   c. Solved
   d. Variability

6. In mathematics, a _____ is a constant multiplicative factor of a certain object. For example, in the expression $9x^2$, the _____ of x^2 is 9.

The object can be such things as a variable, a vector, a function, etc.

   a. 130-30 fund
   b. 100-year flood
   c. 1921 recession
   d. Coefficient

7. In probability theory and statistics, _____ is a measure of the variability or dispersion of a population, a data set, or a probability distribution. A low _____ indicates that the data points tend to be very close to the same value (the mean), while high _____ indicates that the data are 'spread out' over a large range of values.

For example, the average height for adult men in the United States is about 70 inches, with a _____ of around 3 inches.

   a. 130-30 fund
   b. 1921 recession
   c. 100-year flood
   d. Standard deviation

8. Economics:

   - _____, the desire to own something and the ability to pay for it
   - _____ curve, a graphic representation of a _____ schedule
   - _____ deposit, the money in checking accounts
   - _____ pull theory, the theory that inflation occurs when _____ for goods and services exceeds existing supplies
   - _____ schedule, a table that lists the quantity of a good a person will buy it each different price
   - _____ side economics, the school of economics at believes government spending and tax cuts open economy by raising _____

   a. Production
   b. Variability
   c. McKesson ' Robbins scandal
   d. Demand

9. _____ is the business practice where a company inflates its sales figures by forcing more products through a distribution channel than the channel is capable of selling to the world at large. Also known as 'trade loading', this can be the result of a company attempting to inflate its sales figures. Alternatively, it can be a consequence of a poorly managed sales force attempting to meet short term objectives and quotas in a way that is detrimental to the company in the long term.
   a. Gross spread
   b. Financial contagion
   c. Monopoly price
   d. Channel stuffing

10. Discounting is a financial mechanism in which a debtor obtains the right to delay payments to a creditor, for a defined period of time, in exchange for a charge or fee. Essentially, the party that owes money in the present purchases the right to delay the payment until some future date. The _____, or charge, is simply the difference between the original amount owed in the present and the amount that has to be paid in the future to settle the debt.
    a. Reinsurance
    b. Reliability theory
    c. Certified Risk Manager
    d. Discount

11. _____ is the acquisition of goods and/or services at the best possible total cost of ownership, in the right quantity and quality, at the right time, in the right place and from the right source for the direct benefit or use of corporations or individuals, generally via a contract. Simple _____ may involve nothing more than repeat purchasing. Complex _____ could involve finding long term partners - or even 'co-destiny' suppliers that might fundamentally commit one organization to another.

Chapter 13. Supply Chain Coordination

   a. Golden umbrella
   b. Sole proprietorship
   c. Procurement
   d. Pre-emerging markets

12. _____ refers to a business or organization attempting to acquire goods or services to accomplish the goals of the enterprise. Though there are several organizations that attempt to set standards in the _____ process, processes can vary greatly between organizations. Typically the word '_____' is not used interchangeably with the word 'procurement', since procurement typically includes Expediting, Supplier Quality, and Traffic and Logistics (T'L) in addition to _____.
   a. 130-30 fund
   b. 100-year flood
   c. Free port
   d. Purchasing

13. _____ in economics and business is the result of an exchange and from that trade we assign a numerical monetary value to a good, service or asset. If Alice trades Bob 4 apples for an orange, the _____ of an orange is 4 apples. Inversely, the _____ of an apple is 1/4 oranges.
   a. Price war
   b. Price book
   c. Premium pricing
   d. Price

14. _____ is a broad label that refers to any individuals or households that use goods and services generated within the economy. The concept of a _____ is used in different contexts, so that the usage and significance of the term may vary.

Typically when business people and economists talk of _____s they are talking about person as _____, an aggregated commodity item with little individuality other than that expressed in the buy/not-buy decision.

   a. 1921 recession
   b. 130-30 fund
   c. 100-year flood
   d. Consumer

15. _____ is a joint trade and industry body working towards making the grocery sector as a whole more responsive to consumer demand and promote the removal of unnecessary costs from the supply chain.

Chapter 13. Supply Chain Coordination

The _____ movement beginning in the mid-nineties was characterized by the emergence of new principles of collaborative management along the supply chain. It was understood that companies can serve consumers better, faster and at less cost by working together with trading partners.

   a. ACEA agreement
   b. ACCRA Cost of Living Index
   c. AD-IA Model
   d. Efficient Consumer Response

16. In economics, _____ is a rise in the general level of prices of goods and services in an economy over a period of time. When the general price level rises, each unit of currency buys fewer goods and services; consequently, _____ is also a decline in the real value of money--a loss of purchasing power in the medium of exchange which is also the monetary unit of account in the economy. A chief measure of general price-level _____ is the general _____ rate, which is the percentage change in a general price index (normally the Consumer Price Index) over time.
   a. Inflation
   b. Opportunity cost
   c. Economic
   d. Energy economics

17. Collaborative Planning, Forecasting and Replenishment (_____) is a concept that aims to enhance supply chain integration by supporting and assisting joint practices. _____ seeks cooperative management of inventory through joint visibility and replenishment of products throughout the supply chain. Information shared between suppliers and retailers aids in planning and satisfying customer demands through a supportive system of shared information.
   a. CPFR
   b. Delayed differentiation
   c. Demand side
   d. Reverse auction

18. _____ is a concept that aims to enhance supply chain integration by supporting and assisting joint practices. CPFR seeks cooperative management of inventory through joint visibility and replenishment of products throughout the supply chain. Information shared between suppliers and retailers aids in planning and satisfying customer demands through a supportive system of shared information.
   a. Reverse auction
   b. CPFR
   c. Demand side
   d. Collaborative Planning, Forecasting and Replenishment

Chapter 13. Supply Chain Coordination

19. _____ refers to the structured transmission of data between organizations by electronic means. It is used to transfer electronic documents from one computer system to another (ie) from one trading partner to another trading partner. It is more than mere E-mail; for instance, organizations might replace bills of lading and even checks with appropriate _____ messages.

   a. Auction software
   b. E-tailer
   c. Electronic commerce
   d. Electronic data interchange

20. _____ is the process of estimation in unknown situations. Prediction is a similar, but more general term. Both can refer to estimation of time series, cross-sectional or longitudinal data.

   a. 130-30 fund
   b. 1921 recession
   c. Forecasting
   d. 100-year flood

21. The term '_____' gained popularity as a result of the 9/11 Commission Hearings and its report of the United States government's lack of response to information known about the planned terrorist attack on the New York City World Trade Center prior to the event. The resulting commission testimony led to the enactment of several executive orders by President Bush that mandated agencies implement policies to 'share information' across organizational boundaries.

The term '_____' in the information technology lexicon has a long history.

   a. AD-IA Model
   b. ACCRA Cost of Living Index
   c. ACEA agreement
   d. Information sharing

22. _____ is a family of business models in which the buyer of a product provides certain information to a supplier of that product and the supplier takes full responsibility for maintaining an agreed inventory of the material, usually at the buyer's consumption location (usually a store.) A third party logistics provider can also be involved to make sure that the buyer has the required level of inventory by adjusting the demand and supply gaps.

As a symbiotic relationship, _____ makes it less likely that a business will unintentionally become out of stock of a good and reduces inventory in the supply chain.

Chapter 13. Supply Chain Coordination

a. Vendor Managed Inventory
b. Demand-side
c. CPFR
d. Delayed differentiation

23. In molecular kinetic theory in physics, a particle's _____ is a function of seven variables, $f(x,y,z,t;v_x,v_y,v_z)$, which gives the number of particles per unit volume in phase space. It is the number of particles having approximately the velocity (v_x,v_y,v_z) near the place (x,y,z) and time (t). The usual normalization of the _____ is

$$n(x,y,z,t) = \int f \, dv_x \, dv_y \, dv_z$$

$$N(t) = \int n \, dx \, dy \, dz$$

Here, N is the total number of particles and n is the number density of particles - the number of particles per unit volume, or the density divided by the mass of individual particles.

a. 100-year flood
b. 1921 recession
c. 130-30 fund
d. Distribution Function

24. In probability theory and statistics, the _____ or Gaussian distribution is a continuous probability distribution that describes data that clusters around a mean or average. The graph of the associated probability density function is bell-shaped, with a peak at the mean, and is known as the Gaussian function or bell curve.

The _____ can be used to describe, at least approximately, any variable that tends to cluster around the mean.

a. 130-30 fund
b. 100-year flood
c. 1921 recession
d. Normal Distribution

25. which is known as the _____ distribution. When properly scaled and translated, the corresponding cumulative distribution function is known as the error function.

The Gaussian distribution is named for Carl Friedrich Gauss, who used it to analyze astronomical data, and defined the formula for its probability density function.

a. 1921 recession
b. 130-30 fund
c. Standard Normal
d. 100-year flood

26. which is known as the _____. When properly scaled and translated, the corresponding cumulative distribution function is known as the error function.

The Gaussian distribution is named for Carl Friedrich Gauss, who used it to analyze astronomical data, and defined the formula for its probability density function.

a. 130-30 fund
b. 1921 recession
c. Standard Normal Distribution
d. 100-year flood

27. In economics and finance, _____ is the change in total cost that arises when the quantity produced changes by one unit. It is the cost of producing one more unit of a good. Mathematically, the _____ function is expressed as the first derivative of the total cost (TC) function with respect to quantity (Q.)

a. Variable cost
b. Marginal cost
c. Khozraschyot
d. Quality costs

28. _____ is one of the four Ps of the marketing mix. The other three aspects are product, promotion, and place. It is also a key variable in microeconomic price allocation theory.

a. Point of total assumption
b. Pricing
c. Guaranteed Maximum Price
d. Premium pricing

29. The concept was first developed in game theory and consequently zero-sum situations are often called _____s though this does not imply that the concept applies only to what are commonly referred to as games.

Chapter 13. Supply Chain Coordination

For 2-player finite _____s, the different game theoretic Solution concepts of Nash equilibrium, minimax, and maximin all give the same solution. In the solution, players play a mixed strategy.

a. Gordon growth model
b. Cash or share options
c. General purpose technologies
d. Zero-sum game

30. In probability theory and statistics, the _____ (or expectation value or mean and for continuous random variables with a density function it is the probability density -weighted integral of the possible values.

The term '_____' can be misleading.

a. ACEA agreement
b. ACCRA Cost of Living Index
c. AD-IA Model
d. Expected value

31. In statistics, _____ has two related meanings:

- the arithmetic _____
- the expected value of a random variable, which is also called the population _____.

It is sometimes stated that the '_____' _____s average. This is incorrect if '_____' is taken in the specific sense of 'arithmetic _____' as there are different types of averages: the _____, median, and mode. Other simple statistical analyses use measures of spread, such as range, interquartile range, or standard deviation. For a real-valued random variable X, the _____ is the expectation of X. Note that not every probability distribution has a defined _____ (or variance); see the Cauchy distribution for an example.

a. Mean
b. 1921 recession
c. 100-year flood
d. 130-30 fund

32. _____ is a concept with somewhat disparate meanings in several fields. It also has a common meaning which has a loose connection with some of those more definite meanings.

Casually, it is typically used to denote a lack of order, or purpose, or cause.

a. 1921 recession
b. 130-30 fund
c. Randomness
d. 100-year flood

33. In mathematics, _____ are used in the study of chance and probability. They were developed to assist in the analysis of games of chance, stochastic events, and the results of scientific experiments by capturing only the mathematical properties necessary to answer probabilistic questions. Further formalizations have firmly grounded the entity in the theoretical domains of mathematics by making use of measure theory.

a. 1921 recession
b. 130-30 fund
c. 100-year flood
d. Random variables

34. _____ is the a method of technical and economic research of the systems for purpose to optimize a parity between system's consumer functions or properties and expenses to achieve those functions or properties.

This methodology for continuous perfection of production, industrial technologies, organizational structures was developed by Juryj Sobolev in 1948 at the 'Perm telephone factory'

- 1948 Juryj Sobolev - the first success in application of a method analysis at the 'Perm telephone factory'.
- 1949 - the first application for the invention as result of use of the new method.

Today in economically developed countries practically each enterprise or the company use methodology of the kind of functional-cost analysis as a practice of the quality management, most full satisfying to principles of standards of series ISO 9000.

- Interest of consumer not in products itself, but the advantage which it will receive from its usage.
- The consumer aspires to reduce his expenses
- Functions needed by consumer can be executed in the various ways, and, hence, with various efficiency and expenses. Among possible alternatives of realization of functions exist such in which the parity of quality and the price is the optimal for the consumer.

The goal of _____ is achievement of the highest consumer satisfaction of production at simultaneous decrease in all kinds of industrial expenses Classical _____ has three English synonyms - Value Engineering, Value Management, Value Analysis.

a. Staple financing
b. Willingness to pay
c. Monopoly wage
d. Function cost analysis

35. In probability theory, a probability _____ of a random variable is a function which describes the density of probability at each point in the sample space. The probability of a random variable falling within a given set is given by the integral of its density over the set.

A probability _____ is most commonly associated with continuous univariate distributions.

a. Memorylessness
b. Density function
c. Markov blanket
d. Graphical model

36. In probability theory and statistics, the _____ is a discrete probability distribution that expresses the probability of a number of events occurring in a fixed period of time if these events occur with a known average rate and independently of the time since the last event. The _____ can also be used for the number of events in other specified intervals such as distance, area or volume.

The distribution was discovered by Siméon-Denis Poisson and published, together with his probability theory, in 1838 in his work Recherches sur la probabilité des jugements en matières criminelles et matière civile ('Research on the Probability of Judgments in Criminal and Civil Matters'.)

a. 1921 recession
b. Poisson distribution
c. 100-year flood
d. 130-30 fund

37. _____ is a way of expressing knowledge or belief that an event will occur or has occurred. In mathematics the concept has been given an exact meaning in _____ theory, that is used extensively in such areas of study as mathematics, statistics, finance, gambling, science, and philosophy to draw conclusions about the likelihood of potential events and the underlying mechanics of complex systems.

The word _____ does not have a consistent direct definition.

Chapter 13. Supply Chain Coordination

a. 1921 recession
b. 100-year flood
c. 130-30 fund
d. Probability

38. In statistics, _____ indicates the strength and direction of a linear relationship between two random variables. That is in contrast with the usage of the term in colloquial speech, which denotes any relationship, not necessarily linear. In general statistical usage, _____ or co-relation refers to the departure of two random variables from independence.

a. 1921 recession
b. 130-30 fund
c. 100-year flood
d. Correlation

39. The terms 'dependent variable' and '_____' are used in similar but subtly different ways in mathematics and statistics as part of the standard terminology in those subjects. They are used to distinguish between two types of quantities being considered, separating them into those available at the start of a process and those being created by it, where the latter (dependent variables) are dependent on the former (_____s.)

The _____ is typically the variable being manipulated or changed and the dependent variable is the observed result of the _____ being manipulated.

a. ACEA agreement
b. AD-IA Model
c. Independent variable
d. ACCRA Cost of Living Index

40. _____ is a formula for the blocking probability derived from the Erlang distribution to describe the probability of call loss on a group of circuits It is, for example, used in planning telephone networks. The formula was derived by Agner Krarup Erlang and is not limited to telephone networks, since it describes a probability in a queuing system

a. ACCRA Cost of Living Index
b. ACEA agreement
c. AD-IA Model
d. Erlang-B

41. In statistics, decision theory and economics, a _____ is a function that maps an event (technically an element of a sample space) onto a real number representing the economic cost or regret associated with the event.

Chapter 13. Supply Chain Coordination

Less technically, in statistics a _____ represents the loss (cost in money or loss in utility in some other sense) associated with an estimate being 'wrong' (different from either a desired or a true value) as a function of a measure of the degree of wrongness (generally the difference between the estimated value and the true or desired value.)

Both Frequentist and Bayesian statistical theory involve calculating statistics in such a way as to minimize the expected loss observed from being wrong given a set of assumptions about the data and one's _____.

   a. Loss Function
   b. Population modeling
   c. Window function
   d. 100-year flood

42. _____s is the social science that studies the production, distribution, and consumption of goods and services. The term _____s comes from the Ancient Greek oá¼°κονομῖα from oá¼¶κος (oikos, 'house') + vÏŒμος (nomos, 'custom' or 'law'), hence 'rules of the house(hold)'. Current _____ models developed out of the broader field of political economy in the late 19th century, owing to a desire to use an empirical approach more akin to the physical sciences.
   a. Opportunity cost
   b. Energy economics
   c. Inflation
   d. Economic

43. _____ is the level of inventory that minimizes the total inventory holding costs and ordering costs. The framework used to determine this order quantity is also known as Wilson _____ Model. The model was developed by F. W. Harris in 1913.
   a. ACEA agreement
   b. AD-IA Model
   c. ACCRA Cost of Living Index
   d. Economic order quantity

44. _____ is the process of understanding, anticipating and influencing consumer behavior in order to maximize revenue or profits from a fixed, perishable resource This process was first discovered by Dr. Matt H. Keller. The challenge is to sell the right resources to the right customer at the right time for the right price.
   a. Yield management
   b. Coopetition
   c. Freebie marketing
   d. Subscription

Chapter 13. Supply Chain Coordination

45. In microeconomics, _____ is quite simply the conversion of inputs into outputs. It is an economic process that uses resources to create a good or service that is suitable for exchange. This can include manufacturing, storing, shipping, and packaging.
    a. Solved
    b. Production
    c. MET
    d. Red Guards

46. The term _____, 'the state or characteristic of being variable', _____ describes how spread out or closely clustered a set of data is. may be applied to many different subjects:

    - Climate _____
    - Genetic _____
    - Heart rate _____
    - Human _____
    - Solar van
    - Spatial _____
    - Statistical _____
    - _____

    a. Characteristic
    b. Total product
    c. Demand
    d. Variability

ANSWER KEY

Chapter 1
1. d   2. a   3. c   4. d   5. c   6. c   7. d   8. b   9. c   10. d
11. d   12. a   13. d   14. d   15. d   16. b   17. c   18. d   19. b   20. b

Chapter 2
1. d   2. d   3. b

Chapter 3
1. c   2. a   3. b   4. b   5. c   6. a   7. c   8. c   9. d   10. b
11. d   12. d

Chapter 4
1. c   2. b   3. a   4. c   5. d   6. a   7. c   8. b   9. a   10. a
11. d   12. c   13. d   14. d

Chapter 5
1. d   2. b   3. d   4. d   5. d   6. d   7. a   8. d   9. d   10. a
11. a   12. d   13. d   14. b   15. d   16. a   17. a   18. b   19. d   20. a
21. b

Chapter 6
1. d   2. a   3. d   4. b   5. d   6. d   7. a   8. b

Chapter 7
1. b   2. a   3. d   4. d   5. d   6. b   7. b   8. d   9. d   10. d
11. b   12. a   13. d   14. d   15. b   16. d   17. d   18. d   19. b   20. d
21. c   22. d

Chapter 8
1. d   2. a   3. a   4. a   5. c   6. b   7. d   8. d   9. d   10. b
11. b   12. b   13. a   14. c   15. d   16. d   17. a   18. d   19. d   20. d
21. a   22. d   23. a

Chapter 9
1. c   2. d   3. b   4. d   5. a   6. b   7. d   8. b   9. a   10. d
11. a   12. d   13. d   14. b   15. d   16. a   17. c   18. d   19. c

Chapter 10
1. a   2. d   3. a   4. a   5. c   6. d   7. a   8. d   9. a   10. d
11. d   12. d   13. c   14. d   15. c   16. a   17. d   18. a   19. a   20. b
21. b   22. d   23. a   24. d   25. c   26. d

Chapter 11
1. b   2. d   3. d   4. c   5. c   6. d   7. a   8. c   9. a   10. d
11. d   12. d   13. c   14. d   15. d   16. b   17. b   18. b   19. c   20. d
21. d   22. d   23. c

ANSWER KEY

Chapter 12
1. d   2. d   3. a   4. d   5. d   6. d   7. d   8. a   9. c   10. a

Chapter 13
1. d   2. d   3. b   4. d   5. a   6. d   7. d   8. d   9. d   10. d
11. c   12. d   13. d   14. d   15. d   16. a   17. a   18. d   19. d   20. c
21. d   22. a   23. d   24. d   25. c   26. c   27. b   28. b   29. d   30. d
31. a   32. c   33. d   34. d   35. b   36. b   37. d   38. d   39. c   40. d
41. a   42. d   43. d   44. a   45. b   46. d

www.ingramcontent.com/pod-product-compliance
Lightning Source LLC
Chambersburg PA
CBHW081848230426
43669CB00018B/2869